Your Pet and Your Health

How Pets Improve Our Health in This Life—and the Possibility of Meeting Them in the Afterlife

Steve Wohlberg and David DeRose, M.D.

White Horse Media, PO Box 8057, Fresno, CA 93747

To order additional copies of this book, call 1-800-78-BIBLE

White Horse Media
PO Box 8057
Fresno, CA 93747
1-800-78-BIBLE
www.whitehorsemedia.com

Other fascinating books by Steve Wohlberg:

From Hollywood to Heaven
Truth Left Behind
End Time Delusions
Demons in Disguise
The Antichrist Chronicles
Exposing Harry Potter and Witchcraft
Solving the Mystery of Death
The Hot Topic of Hell
The Millennium

Page Composition by Ken McFarland
Cover design by Steve Miljatovic

ISBN: 0-9722233-6-3

Contents

An Angel Must Have Done It!

In May of 2003, Steve Wohlberg received this amazing letter concerning his book *Will My Pet Go to Heaven?* which is reproduced in its entirety in Section 3 of this book. Reader responses to that book will be found on various other pages.

I rarely do this type of thing, but I need you to know what a blessing your book has been to me and my 9-year-old daughter. It has been a horrible year. I lost my job a year ago due to the ailing health of both me and my daughter. We suspect sick home syndrome and toxic mold and yet have no money for testing. We filed bankruptcy in November and still cannot stay on top of regular living expenses. Our home is now in foreclosure.

We tried to move into an apartment but were declined due to bankruptcy. The washing machine broke over two months ago, and we are unable to replace it. Time at the laundromat is very depressing with a child in tow, after I have been a professional in corporate America all my life. I broke down last week and finally filed for food stamps. I was humiliated. Where is my God? (I promise the story gets better). My daughter left to go see her father in Missouri last week, and when I came home, her dog MacTavish—little Cairn Terrier—had been sick all over the carpet of the house we are desperately trying to sell to recoup equity and recover from this year.

Irritated at the call I received from the agent about the house being shown when the dog had an "accident," I went to yell at my dog and found him lethargic and shaking. . . . I am sure you have read a million of these stories, so I will get straight to the point. Mac got worse and worse—what could I do? I had no money for a vet, but this is a family member. Finally, I prayed and decided to take him in. The vet needed x-rays and tests, and ultimately surgery, as he appeared to have an intestinal blockage. I can't! I cried and cried but knew he was suffering.

They put him to sleep, and I agonized over what to tell my sweet daughter who has lost so much already this year. This little guy sleeps with her every night—even swims in the pool with her and her friends! When I arrived at the airport, my stomach was hurting thinking about her pain. I went into a little shop to get a soda, and there next to the cooler sat your book *Will My Pet Go to Heaven?* My heart began to pound. . . . I picked it up and read the back—then I saw the price, which is a lot of money to a person with no job, but I decided God put it there, so I will BUY it! I looked all over the store for another copy and couldn't find one . . . how odd. I went to the counter and put down my soda and the book, and the cashier said to me, "Oh, you can have that book, because someone just left it here this morning!"

I stepped out of the store with tears running down my face. How can the God I have been questioning and even swearing at many times this year be so merciful on THIS issue as to place this book in my hands to comfort the one thing I have and love so much, my little girl? Does He care that much about the little things? Yes! He really does.

When I arrived home, I held my daughter and gave her the bad news. Oh, how we both cried! Then I told her the story about the book. . . . I took it out of my purse, and we began reading together. Madison said to me, with tears running down her face, "Mommy, it was an angel that left that book for us, wasn't it?" I said, "Yes, Honey, it sure was."

So I want to thank you for writing it and let you know how it has blessed a family walking through the fire and trying to keep the faith. MacTavish is in our hearts, and it's sad to see his bowl and toys. However, through his death has come a strange peace. It was almost as if God used him to say to me, "I do care, Kim, hang in there and show your daughter that I do not promise us a life without loss or sorrow but rather that I will be with you while you muddle your way through."

May God richly bless you and your family for following His direction to write a book that An Angel from Heaven put in my hands at the hardest time in my life. Thank you again.

Kimberley Childress Muench
Texas

1. Furry Friends at Ground Zero

There is no psychiatrist in the world like a puppy licking your face.
—BEN WILLIAMS (1877-1964)

The week of September 11, 2001, has been called "The week that changed America"[1] During the days that followed that fateful Tuesday morning, millions of Americans watched—over and over again on CBS, NBC, and CNN—the images of hijacked planes that became guided missiles ramming into buildings, of doomed people jumping out of flaming windows, and of noble fireman who risked their lives or lost them trying to save others.

Yet something else went almost unnoticed. It wasn't reported by Peter Jennings on ABC's *World News Tonight*—or by any other news anchor. Nevertheless, it was real—and extremely important—to those whose hearts were touched. It was the story of the incredible comfort that paws, whiskers, and animal tongues brought to human beings at Ground Zero.

As we begin this book highlighting the benefits of pets to people in this life—and then explore the possibility of meeting them again in the afterlife—we want to start by revealing the moving account of how friendly animals brought comfort to shell-shocked humans in the immediate aftermath of one of the most stressful events in U.S. history.

I love a dog. He does nothing for political reasons.
—WILL ROGERS (1879-1935)

Nanette Winter, Director of Psychological Services for Northstar Industries in New York, has often served as a volunteer for a wonderful organization called Therapy Dogs International, Inc. (TDI). Founded in 1976, TDI has for many years trained and sent animals to bring warmth, love, and healing to people in need. Shortly after the Twin Towers collapsed, TDI workers—along with their dogs—came to New York to help. Nanette was one of those volunteers who received an urgent call to assist near Ground Zero. Here's her story:

"As a therapist, I have used dogs in my work for over twenty years. I firmly believe that animals have a profoundly positive impact on our physical and emotional health and well-being. I watch as my dogs turn that belief into reality each and every day.

"Following the tragic events of September 11, 2001, I received a call from TDI to volunteer at the Family Assistance Center on Pier 94 in New York City. Despite my many years of using my

dogs to help soothe and calm others, this would be my biggest crisis intervention experience ever. It was an honor to be able to help in this most magical and rewarding way.

One reason the dog has so many friends:
He wags his tail instead of his tongue.
—AUTHOR UNKNOWN

"A quote by Allen Schoen and Pam Proctor has been a guiding principle for me in my work. In their book entitled *Love, Miracles, and Animal Healing*, they state, 'By their very presence in our midst, animals awaken in us the desire to respond and to love.' The work that our Therapy Dogs accomplished in New York City really exemplified this, and it brought to the forefront the profound and compelling bond between humans and animals. As our dogs were approached by each person, the dogs instantly responded with compassion and love—no questions, no tough demands. Their touch brought warmth and comfort to many broken hearts. They helped people relax—perhaps even to open up a bit and let the words, or the tears, begin.

"For others, the dogs brought a smile to their faces—a brief but important respite from the shocking pain and sorrow. For the children, they brought joy and comfort—a safe bridge between child and adult—a way to connect, a chance amidst the confusion and sadness to laugh and to play. For the other volunteers and relief workers, our dogs were invaluable in providing a break from the intensity of emotion. They brought a sense of normalcy to these abnormal times and simplicity amid the chaos. And they created a cozy sense of security and warmth throughout the Center.

"In short, our dogs have played a valuable role in helping others begin the healing process after the tragedy of September 11. They have also helped all of us to put things in perspective and to reconnect with life's simple and most important values. It never ceases to amaze me how quickly and effectively our dogs can touch others' hearts and help them to heal. Despite my years of training, experience, and education, I will always believe that sometimes the most effective kind of therapy begins with a cold, wet nose and ends with the wag of a tail. I know that in New York City, there are many who would agree."[2]

Sarah Sypniewski, a 23-year-old caseworker for the Red Cross, was also assigned to work at the Family Assistance Center at Pier 94 in New York City just a few weeks after the World Trade Center was destroyed. Her task was to evaluate the victims who came to the center and to give general guidance as to where they might receive assistance in those days of crisis. Day by day, as those with needs came to her for help, she had a hard time holding herself together, much less helping others. Yet as a result of TDI's therapy dogs—who showed up every day at the pier—she was able to make it through. Daily, the dogs approached both workers and victims, bringing a sense of hope, relief, and friendliness into an otherwise almost unbearable situation.

On the day before she left New York for her return flight to California, she penned this memorable poem to honor the gentle animals that so deeply soothed her soul:

Paws Amidst Pain

Dedicated to the therapy dogs at Pier 94 in NYC who worked so hard
responding to the human mess of 9/11, particularly to my special friend, Wusel.
Thank you, dogs and humans, for your undying love.

*The hours upon hours you pad through these paths of pain
are the hours you help us see the light through the pouring rain.
You never falter, never fail, and always call to mind
the joy and inspiration that's sometimes hard to find.*

*As we muddle through the wreckage that's half hope and half despair,
You stand by like an anchor, tail wagging in the air.
With every touch you heal us, from fur to human heart,
solace in each stroke, you prevent our falling apart.
You never complain, and though you cry, you do not show your tears,
you swallow them back, hold your post, and calm so many fears.*

*Your spirit penetrates our beings right into our souls,
you let us touch and talk to you as we try to fill the holes.*

*There are times we want to just give up and head back to our homes,
and there you are with pricked-up ears, and then we're not alone.
You sigh, surrender, and knowingly roll onto your back;
"Here's my tummy—you can have it . . . just give me a snack."*

You do so much for us we just can't do ourselves,
you specialize in soul-speak that never ceases to delve
straight into the place we do not talk about.
You let us cry and let us laugh and get all of it out.

So before I go, I want to say I hope you know the truth:
You saved me every single day,

I survived because of you.[3]

—BY SARAH SYPNIEWSKI
L.A. COUNTY PROGRAM COORDINATOR
NATIONAL READINESS AND RESPONSE CORPS
WRITTEN ON 11/02/01

2. Terrific Tales of Animal Heroism

The average dog is a nicer person than the average person.
—ANDREW A. ROONEY

Derek, a Golden Retriever, is truly a "lifesaver." Doctors agree that on a number of occasions, he saved his human companion, Steve Wilson, from probable death or disability. Derek somehow has the uncanny ability to sense when Steve is about to experience myocardial ischemia—lack of blood supply to his heart. And on a number of occasions, Derek's barks, whimpers, and prodding stimulated Steve to remove himself from precarious situations. Were those situations really all that dangerous? Consider this: The only two times Steve ignored his dog, he suffered a heart attack.

No one can explain how Derek does it. Some think he senses when an experience is particularly stressful to his companion. Others conjecture the retriever's keen sense of smell hones in on faint odors emanating from Steve's body that indicate early changes in heart blood supply or elevated stress hormone levels. Steve Wilson can't explain it either, but there's no question in his mind: *He owes his life to his dog.*

Although Derek's life-saving abilities might seem highly unusual, his story is only the proverbial tip of the iceberg as to documented cases of animal heroics. Anna, an aged Siamese cat, defended Susan Burleson from a burglar who broke into Susan's apartment by pouncing upon the intruder and mercilessly clawing his neck and face. Hugo, a burly Rottweiler, dragged Rachel, his paraplegic companion, to safety after she was knocked unconscious in a car wreck. Shadow, a black Quarter Horse, intervened between two-year-old Dusty and a raging bull, sparing the toddler's life.

One of the greatest compilers of animal rescue stories is the world-famous producer of pet food—Heinz Pet Products. Since 1954, Heinz has granted an annual "Dog Hero of the Year" award for noble feats of heroism. From among numerous submissions into the contest describing incredible life-and-death dramas, the following courageous canines were among those who won the yearly prize:

Mehlville, Missouri, 1959: Lady, a mixed breed, frantically searched for help and brought back two telephone linemen to rescue a 3-year-old boy who was sinking in a muddy swamp.

Euless, Texas, 1968: When his 2-year-old master wandered away from home and started playing in the midst of traffic, Ringo, also a mixed breed, barked and ran circles around the boy to divert oncoming cars.

John's Island, South Carolina, 1973: A 14-month-old Saint Bernard named Budweiser saved one of his owner's grandchildren, then another, by dragging them by their shirts from a burning house.

Cleveland, Ohio, 1980: Woodie, a mixed breed, broke his hip when he leaped from an eighty-foot cliff to rescue Ray, his owner's fiancé, who fell from the cliff and landed face down in a river. The wounded dog kept Ray's face above water until help arrived.

It's character that counts. We should show unconditional love to our families, loyalty to our friends, and always seek to protect them from harm. When we fully attain such an exalted character, we will finally exhibit the normal traits of a dog.

—AUTHOR UNKNOWN

Dickenson, North Carolina, 1986: Together, Champ, a terrier, and Buddy, a mixed breed, led their owners to a nearby warehouse, where an injured truck driver was trapped beneath a 2,680-pound earth mover tire.

Watsonville, California, 1989: During the San Francisco earthquake, Reona the Rottweiler saved a frightened 5-year-old epileptic girl by pushing the child aside just before a microwave oven fell from the top of a refrigerator. The dog then calmed the young girl and prevented her from having a seizure.

Tullahoma, Tennessee, 1992: When Sparky's burly 227-pound owner, Bo, collapsed from a heart attack during a morning walk, this 130-pound yellow Labrador Retriever dragged his master nearly two hundred yards. Bo made it to the hospital just in time for his condition to be stabilized.

Imperial Beach, California, 1993: During large-scale flooding in Southern California's Tijuana River valley, Weela's repeated heroism over a three-month period saved thirty people, twenty-nine dogs, thirteen horses, and one cat—all of whom otherwise might have perished in the flood.

Tucson, Arizona, 1996: Despite being shot five times by a home invader, Brandy kept up her fight and chased the attacker out, saving the life of his owner.

LaBelle, Florida, 2002: Two-year-old Blue, an Australian Blue Heeler, rescued his 85-year-old owner from a vicious alligator attack and survived numerous injuries from the dangerous encounter.[4]

Indeed, the world is replete with stories about pets saving the lives of their human companions. These miraculous tales involve a wide spectrum of God's creatures—dogs, cats, horses, birds, dolphins, ocean turtles, and even pigs. It's true. Literally thousands of human beings have been personally awed to see their beloved pets courageously intervene on their behalf.

Bumper stickers and highway signs often say, "Jesus Saves."

In a far more limited but just as real way, sometimes animals do, too.

3. Lassie Can Lengthen Your Life

Believe it or not, the secret to growing old gracefully, healthily and even happily may be lying at your feet and licking itself. Research has shown that pets—or even the presence of animals—have indisputable medical benefits. From lowering blood pressure to easing anxiety and depression, Fido and Kitty are more effective than much of what medical science has in its arsenal.

—THE SUNDAY TIMES, DECEMBER 9, 2001

Janie, a Golden Retriever, waltzed into the room of a patient at Cedars-Sinai Medical Center who had refused to talk with anyone for weeks and did something no medical treatment had been able to do. She put her paws on the edge of the bed, and the patient leaned over, stroked Janie's ears, and began talking. The scene astonished the attending physician and underscored a growing interest among health-care professionals in what is now being referred to as "the healing power of pets."[5]

"Pooch Power: Researchers Document How Pets Keep People Healthy" was the title of an ABC News report.[6] "It's an up-and-coming field," says Lana Kaiser, a physician, veterinarian, and professor at Michigan State University. Dr. Kaiser is also the driving force behind the "Human-Animal Bond Initiative," which has sponsored three national conferences on the Michigan campus bringing researchers together from across North America. Their motto is, "Cuddle a Critter and Call Me in the Morning," Kaiser says.

While animal heroics often make headlines, a growing array of research suggests that dogs, cats, horses, and other four-legged companions assist us in daily living by reducing stress, lowering blood pressure, easing loneliness, aiding the recovery efforts of accident victims, counteracting depression, and promoting general well-being in humans. Thus, dogs are not only man's best friend, but good medicine for what ails us. In fact, in many cases, Fido may work better than Tylenol.

The Delta Society, an organization promoting the animal-human bond, has for many years funded research "on how animals affect health and well-being."[7] Founded in 1977, one of the society's stated goals is to "expand awareness of the positive effect animals can have on human health and development."

Dr. Bonnie Beaver, professor in the Department of Small Animal Medicine and Surgery at the Texas A&M University College of Veterinary Medicine, has added her much-respected voice to the growing chorus of pets-are-good-for-us documentation. Throughout her years of

working with animals, she has compiled a long list of studies proving that pets are health-promoting indeed.[8]

A wide variety of research and documentation has revealed that:

- Pet owners have lower cholesterol levels than non-owners.

- Heart attack victims who own pets survive longer than those who don't.

- Pet owners are generally in better physical condition, because they spend more time outdoors exercising Rover.

- Pets provide therapeutic touch.

- Pet ownership is linked to lower blood pressure.

- Pet owners have better psychological well-being.

- Pets improve children's reading scores, capacity for empathy, and perhaps their I.Q.

- Pets help combat allergies. (When children are exposed at a young age to animals, immunities are built up which actually help prevent allergies.)

- One hundred senior citizens on Medicare who owned dogs made 21 percent fewer visits to their doctor than those without dogs.

Thus Max and Kitty are good for baby, junior, mom, dad, grandma, and grandpa. So why fret about a few dog or cat hairs on the sofa if our pets can add life to our days and length to our years?

Beyond the above-mentioned blessings, Dr. David DeRose has discovered three additional health benefits of owning a critter:

1. Pets provide a social dimension that can improve our life and health. Described as "the bond," the intimate and joyful relationships formed between humans and their animal cohabitants definitely become health-enhancing—especially for senior citizens who crave warmth and friendship.

2. Animals are in touch with their environment and the needs of their bodies to a much greater degree than we humans typically are. By watching the good examples of our pets, we can be inspired to change our lifestyle in ways that enhance our own health.

3. Just like us, most pets have good qualities as well as some that are less desirable. Surprisingly, even their sometimes objectionable characteristics can cause us to take a fresh look at areas in our own lives that need changing. By doing so, we can be motivated to make healthy changes that no human could ever inspire us to consider.

Indeed, when you look at all the health benefits of pets, they may be one of the most under-prescribed therapeutic agents in the world.

In the pages that follow, Dr. DeRose will prove these statements by walking you through some of the exciting research that links pet ownership with improved health. Plus, he'll give you more reasons to be enthusiastic about your animal companions.

However, as a doctor, he has also seen another side and has viewed cases where animals have brought harm to humans. You yourself—or a close family member or friend—may have a pet "horror story" seared into your mind (or buried in your subconscious). This doesn't undermine the value of our fine furred and feathered friends. However, it does point out that there are some potential pitfalls in pet ownership. Dr. DeRose takes a look at these as well—for it's only as you make appropriate pet choices for your own circumstances that you can fully tap into their healing power.

Bottom line: The latest research proves that pets *are* good for us—when precautions are taken. For those who love their animals, the risks and responsibilities are well worth it, paying big dividends.

Why not own one today?

Readers Respond . . .
. . . to *Will My Pet Go to Heaven?*

I just finished reading *Will My Pet Go to Heaven?* and must say that it is the best book on the subject I have ever read. We lost our Mollie on September 5, 1999, and I can truly sympathize with you and your wife and know of your pain and grief. Rudi Ann joined our lives on September 21, 2000. She is a Jack Russell Terrier/Rat Terrier mix. She looks an awful lot like Jax and Rerun! I think that's another reason why your book touched me so. Thank you so much for writing this book!
God Bless!
Lori Whittenberger

Dear Steve, You just cannot imagine what a gift of peace you have brought to my soul, and I just had to tell you how much I appreciate the fact that you wrote this book. The precious pets I live with are my family. I may live alone (the only human), but I am anything but alone, and with my pets around, I am never lonely. May God bless you for the joy you are sharing with other pet lovers.
Sincerely,
Loretta R. Young

Hi Steve . . . it has been two months now since my little companion, Sarah, died. All I can say about your book is AMEN! What wonderful insights you have presented into the love God has for us. . . . It breaks my heart when I see or hear about people mistreating any animal, but especially the little friends that they have been entrusted with. I loved all the side notes you included and the different quotations, including the ones about a horse. . . . Thank you for going way beyond the loss of a pet. May God bless you, your wife Kristin, and little "Rerun" for the ministry you have shared.
Blessings,
Pat

4. Unleashing the Power of the Bond

Old dog Tray is ever faithful;
Grief can not drive him away;
He is gentle, he is kind—
I shall never, never find
A better friend than old dog Tray!

—STEPHEN COLLINS FOSTER (1826-1864)

What do you do with an at-risk kid who has problems even showing up at school? If you ask Jennifer Wise, she'll probably say, "Get him involved with animals." Jennifer heads up the innovative "Kids and Canines" program at the Dorothy Thomas Exceptional Center.[9] Located in the Tampa Bay community of Carrolwood, the program gives selected truant high school students the responsibility of training service dogs.

The creative strategy is paying big dividends throughout Hillsborough County. Teenagers' lives change as they work with the even-tempered Golden Retrievers. The students consistently improve in school attendance and academic performance. For example, one of the student trainers went from chronic truant to student council member and peer mediator. Community residents with disabilities are additional beneficiaries, receiving well-trained assistance dogs.

The benefits accruing to these youth owe to what researchers have called "the animal-human bond" or simply "the bond." These terms refer to the intimate relationship that often forms between humans and their companion animals. A number of scientific studies have looked at the far-reaching implications of long-term human-animal relationships. Position papers and review articles have summarized these research insights, websites have disseminated the information, and popular books have distilled and illustrated the scientific findings. An entire group of veterinarians exists whose members especially champion the importance of "the bond." They call themselves The American Association of Human-Animal Bond Veterinarians (AAHABV).[10]

Pets are far more than mere consumers of our affection and care. Overall, the research indicates that human-pet interactions offer profound benefits to humans—regardless of age or ethnicity. For example, consider a sampling of the benefits that have been linked to the human-animal bond across the age span.[11, 12, 13, 14]

In Childhood and Adolescence

- Increases self-respect
- Reduces loneliness
- Helps autistic children to connect better with their surroundings

15

- Fosters sensitivity, nurturing, and other humanitarian attitudes
- Provides emotional stability for foster children
- Promotes responsibility
- Helps develop empathy
- Improves physical and verbal skills in developmentally challenged youth
- Buffers the effects of stress in traumatized children

In Young and Mid-Adulthood

- Reduces minor health problems
- Improves socialization
- Lowers blood pressure in the face of stress
- Decreases anxiety and despair in psychiatric institutions
- Helps patients cope with cancer

In Older Adulthood

- Enhances quality of life
- Improves survival following a heart attack
- Fosters appropriate social behavior in the mentally impaired
- Helps combat depression in seniors who lack human social support
- Increases adherence to intensive treatment regimens such as cardiac rehabilitation
- Reduces loneliness
- Improves appetite in under-eating patients with Alzheimer's Disease

How can you tap into this long list of benefits? What can you do to unleash the power of the bond in your own life? Of course, it all starts with inviting a pet to share part of your life (if you haven't already done so). However, the mere presence of an animal in your home or apartment does not ensure benefit. A pet with which you seldom interact likely offers you little benefit from the power of the bond. Just as with human social relations, the human-animal bond appears to be fostered best by a critical element—spending time together.

Therefore, evaluate your level of interaction with your pets. If you have one or more companion animals but don't think you're getting any health benefits, why not make more of an effort to experience "the bond?" Get more involved with your pet. Take the dog for a walk. Buy some new toys and play with your cat. Change the environment in your aquarium and watch how the fish respond.

What if you're not a pet lover—or if you love animals but your health care professional has made you promise to keep your distance because of allergies or an impaired immune system? These are important issues. First, I'd never advise that you disregard your doctor's advice. Second, if the very thought of a pet raises your blood pressure—then step back and ask yourself seriously if you may be over-reacting.

I find that many people who can't imagine having a dog or a cat may be very comfortable with the idea of having fish or some other lower-maintenance companion. Although fish don't typically conjure up warm, fuzzy emotions, research suggests that they, too, provide health benefits. For example, studies indicate that gazing at fish in an aquarium relaxes both mind and body, thus relieving stress.

In other words, question your own resistance to having a pet. Perhaps a few bad experiences with one or more species have impaired your objectivity when it comes to the benefits of companion animals. If so, you might want to take a second look and reconsider the matter. The truth is that millions of normal human beings just like you have discovered tremendous benefits from having animals around. Maybe you should try having just one—a small dog or cat. You might like it.

Asking these questions is probably more important for some than for others. Current research about "the bond" suggests that those with the fewest supportive social connections have the greatest need for interaction with animals. In other words, those who don't have many friends stand to get the greatest benefit from opening their hearts to a loving and loyal four-legged companion. If you're lonely, try visiting a local pound or animal shelter and saving the life of a dog or cat on death row. Most likely, in time, you'll be glad you did. Even if you feel that you don't have the time or energy for a pet—think again. Many times our energy level and enthusiasm are low because of depressive tendencies. Pets can be mood elevators. They pick us up and make us smile.

You may be surrounded by people—yet still lack nurturing support. If you are dealing with a serious illness like cancer or AIDS, your normally supportive friends and relatives may be at a loss to know how to provide true support. Companion animals, with their loving, unconditional acceptance, can provide a powerful emotional boost—especially in tough times. In fact, cases are known of people on the verge of suicide who decided to drop the razor, drive away from the bridge, or put the pills away because of Fido's friendliness or the purrs of Fluffy.

Having said all this, I must admit, however, that for certain people, having animals around may not be what they need at this time in their lives. In this light, if your spouse isn't ready, don't browbeat him or her into embracing a Great Dane. I didn't write this chapter to provide ammunition for your latest argument for owning a pet, especially if it upsets a human relationship with a significant other. If your spouse or roommate really doesn't want an animal, don't be pushy, or you may pay too high a price.

Still, the benefits of the bond are so far reaching that it behooves us all to ask the question: Am I missing some—or all—of this powerful, healing influence in my life? If you answer in the affirmative, don't mourn your loss. Rejoice in your new insight—and do something about it. Plenty of animals out there are just waiting for you to become the most important person in their lives.

While not exactly people like us, animals have feelings, too. They get lonely, frightened, and suffer greatly when they lack food, warmth, friendship, and love. Some animal out there may need to be rescued—by you. If you do, you may find they will return the favor by *rescuing you* from depression and loneliness as well.

5. Animals and Allergies

Cats regard people as warm-blooded furniture.
—JACQUELYN MITCHARD, AUTHOR OF THE DEEP END OF THE OCEAN

Within moments of walking into Fran's house, Richard's watering eyes, running nose, and impending sneeze told him he was in feline territory. Richard always liked cats—but don't give him a kitten on his next birthday. His extreme allergies to these beloved pets have eliminated them from his wish list.

How do we deal with pets when it seems they're often implicated in allergic diseases? First, we need to get *all* the facts—and these facts are not as straightforward as some would lead us to believe.

When someone is allergic to a class of animals—like cats—it doesn't necessarily take a huge amount of exposure to trigger a reaction. Consider a study performed at the famous Karolinska Hospital in Stockholm, Sweden.[15] Researchers there, under the direction of Dr. Catarina Almqvist, identified over four hundred grade-school children with a unique profile. Each of them was being treated for asthma and had a documented allergy to cats, yet not one of them had a cat in their home. In fact, ninety-two of these children had absolutely no contact with any furred pets over the study's three-week time period.

However, the researchers made an interesting observation. If any of the students were in a schoolroom where over 18 percent of their non-allergic classmates had cats, they were more likely to have measurable decreases in lung function, increased days with asthma symptoms, and greater use of asthma medications. All told, cat-allergic children sitting in schoolrooms and surrounded by a significant number of cat owners had nine times the risk of worsened asthma, compared to similarly predisposed children who were not around so many other kids who owned a feline.

One implication of this study is that many people have exquisitely sensitive pet allergies. Presumably, even the cat dander on their classmates' clothing was enough to produce measurable ill health effects. Granted, these classroom situations provide relatively low levels of allergen exposure. However, the amount of allergens in the air is by no means insignificant. By actual measurement, the same Swedish research group found that cat owners' clothing indeed carries pet allergens into the school environment—and that those allergens are subsequently dispersed naturally into the classroom air.

Studies like this, documenting the profound potential for pet-related allergies, have caused some to conclude that, despite the positive benefits discussed earlier, they would rather relegate animals to someone else's house, to a pet store, to the streets, or at least to being out of sight. However, such conclusions are both hasty and often unwarranted.

19

On the other hand, another body of research literature suggests that pets in the home may actually *decrease* the risk of allergic problems (including asthma) in some children—as well as adults. University of Bergen (Norway) researcher Dr. Cecilie Svanes and colleagues also looked at the impact of childhood pet ownership on adult allergies, in the multi-national European Community Respiratory Health Survey.[16] They found that people who had a dog in childhood were less likely to develop common allergies later in life (such as sensitivities to cats, grasses, or house-dust mites). Children from allergically predisposed families also appeared to benefit if they grew up with cats in the home. As adults, those individuals were less prone to allergies.

One theory is that these childhood encounters with animals stimulates the body to develop certain "Special Forces" defenders called "IgG antibodies" which protect humans against inhaled pet proteins. These antibodies are like little safety features that help prevent the triggering of allergies.

Another theory proposes that pets expose a child's respiratory system to a number of germs and related compounds that may actually have long-term favorable effects. As strange as that may sound, there is strong evidence for this. The Swiss researcher, Dr. Charlotte Braun-Fahrländer, is a leading proponent of the "hygiene hypothesis," which suggests that growing up in cleaner, pet-free, more germ-free environments may actually *foster* the development of allergies and asthma because the human body does not develop enough Special Forces to resist these problems.

The bottom line is that there are a multitude of factors that may influence development of allergies—both in childhood as well as in later life. From the information at hand, it seems unwarranted to exclude pets from the home simply because of fear that allergies might develop. However, every case is unique, and there may be some compelling situations where certain types of pets might be ill-advised in certain homes. If you have such questions, consult with your doctor and ask if there are health issues of which you should be aware—or research evidence to cause concern. In such cases, you always want to be guided by facts and the reasonable counsel of a trained professional.

If you know you're already allergic to a certain species of animal, yet you really want to own one as a pet, you'll likely need to apply one or more strategies before you can coexist with those particular creatures without undue discomfort. The strategy most often employed is over-the-counter or prescription medication. This is only a short-term solution—it does nothing to influence the allergy itself.

You'll get more mileage if you can keep your exposure down to the particular substance that causes the allergy. For example, try a short-haired dog, as opposed to a long-haired one. Additionally, consider seeing an allergist for *immunotherapy* or "allergy shots." With this help, in time, you can actually build up a tolerance to the pets you love.

Here's another important point: Even if you have documented allergies to one or more animal species, *the problem may not lie wholly with the animals.* I have had many patients over the years tell me that their lifestyle habits significantly influenced the severity of their allergies. In other words, even a pet-allergic person may be able to function with little or no symptoms—even around a type of pet to which they are allergic—simply by making certain health-related changes in their daily lives. Based on responses from my patients and insights from medical literature, I advocate five promising lifestyle strategies to help foster the happy state of enjoying your pet without suffering from allergies:

1. Drink more pure, soft water.
2. Leave off alcohol.

3. Try avoiding dairy products for one month.

4. Increase your outdoor physical exercise.

5. Increase the amount of fresh air circulating through your home.

Some years ago a patient of mine, Richard Boston, enthusiastically strode over to me at a wedding reception. He wanted to make sure he thanked me for how I had helped him to overcome his allergies. Richard explained that the remarkable improvement came as a result of following my instructions to drink more water. As much as I would like to take credit for this amazing bit of medical wisdom, I must admit that my water advocacy was not specifically allergy-related at the time. Until that day at the wedding reception, I had never thought that water drinking could help prevent symptoms of allergies, but in his case, it seemed to have worked!

My interest in the therapeutic implications of this simple beverage increased when a number of Richard's family members talked with me at the same reception. Each not only confirmed his story but added that their own allergies also had been helped by more liberal water consumption. Of course, this interesting family report surely does not constitute scientific proof of anything. However, the experience at least caused me to make a mental note of the association.

Since most of my patients could stand to drink more water for other reasons, I've felt free to share with them this anecdotal report. My comfort level in discussing water intake in the context of allergies has also been increased by bone fide research that has found a connection between skin allergic conditions and both hard water and higher water chlorine content.[17, 18] Drinking more pure, soft water may indeed help allergic conditions. Will it help your pet allergy? Perhaps—but it may have more to do with the fact that your increased water intake is now replacing other harmful fluids that may contribute to stirring up your allergies.

One of those fluids is alcohol. A body of scientific research now suggests that alcoholic beverages may predispose to allergy development, as well as increasing established allergic problems.[19] Both moderate and heavy alcohol users tend to have increased amounts of another substance called IgE, which can contribute to allergies. Are you on the fence when it comes to the pros and cons of alcohol drinking? On top of other medically proven benefits to your liver and brain, if you have allergies, I would suggest that the balance tips in favor of total abstinence. Try it. Give yourself a couple of months and see if you notice any difference, especially around furry pets. You may be pleasantly surprised by the improvement, just as my friend Richard Boston was surprised by the benefits of drinking more water.

There is no question that dairy products are common causes of allergy and intolerance. What is more difficult to say is whether the presence of dairy can accentuate other preexisting allergies, such as those to pollens, pets, or dust. While I can't make a compelling case for dairy avoidance from anything I've reviewed in the medical research literature, I can say that many of my patients over the years have told me that their allergies to *other things* improved dramatically when they removed dairy from their diets. That cumulative testimony has encouraged me to spread the word to other patients, many of whom have also reported good results. Let's face it: If skipping milk products might be the difference between enjoying pets and being miserable around them, a trial of a dairy-free regimen is worth it for many.

However, avoidance of obvious dairy products may not be a panacea. Some people forgo major dairy products with little or no benefit. To really give yourself a fair trial of a dairy-free diet, you have to be a bit more careful and read labels. It's simply not enough to switch from cow's milk to soymilk on your cereal and to pass on those cheesy pizzas and ice cream. In reality, one needs to exclude all things with hidden dairy ingredients. When you look at the labels of certain foods, here are some of the normally unrecognized ingredients that betray dairy's presence: Whey, casein, caseinate, lactalbumin, lactose, and milk solids. Believe it or not, these smaller, hidden ingredients may also contribute to allergies.

Beside the potential impact of our daily choices of food and beverages, other lifestyle factors can play a role in dealing with allergies—to pets as well as to other allergens. I've had a number of patients tell me that regular physical exercise is a significant factor in decreasing their allergic symptoms. Because of its broad range of health-giving effects, it is prudent for each of us to make physical activity a priority. If you've been lacking motivation, and you have pet allergies, why not give it a try? Increase your exercise, and see if it makes any difference.

Keeping fresh air circulating throughout your house is definitely also a winning strategy. The bottom line is that anything that can decrease the amount of pet dander in the air you breathe everyday is likely to help. This can range from something as sophisticated as installing a high-efficiency air filter in your home to something as simple as keeping your windows open more frequently to let heaven's breezes blow in.

I know that you may enjoy cuddling with Rover or Felix, but when allergy is part of the picture, it's better to try to sleep in a different room from your four-legged friends. Better still is to keep your pet entirely out of the sleeping room—even when you are not in there. You may be surprised at the difference this makes.

Fresh air is one of the neglected health-giving agents. Fortunately, our pets may help us make this easily overlooked commodity a priority. Consider Rocco, my brother Ken's Jack Russell Terrier. This dog epitomizes perpetual motion. If he's inside, there's something more exciting outside. After being outdoors for a few minutes, Rocco usually decides its time to come back in.

Now, I can't imagine Rocco going even a few hours without getting fresh air. It doesn't matter what the temperature is—he wants to get out. Perhaps it's the freedom of the outdoors that he loves. Maybe it's the stimulation he gets from his own little doggy war game—chasing squirrels. However, I surmise that he and millions of other pets drawn to the outdoors are lured—at least in part—by the promise of fresh air. The truth is, outside air is really good for us!

Scientists have discovered what I surmise our pets knew all along; namely, that fresh air is abundant in negatively charged ions that have mood-elevating effects. Fresh air also helps your lungs function better by improving the natural cleansing action of tiny lung hairs called *cilia*. Researchers have also found that fresh air improves long-term human performance. Athletes who exercised out of doors in the fresh air and sunshine made greater strength improvement than those who followed the same regimen within four walls.

Perhaps this provides another insight into why your retriever is not content walking with you on an indoor treadmill—or why your cat won't settle for the same routine. Animals love to be out of doors, and this may result in one of their greatest gifts to their owners. *They motivate us* to get off the couch, away from the TV, and into that healing outdoor environment.

In summary, a good amount of research—combined with practical experience—suggests that children may actually gain allergy protection from growing up around animals. And even if adults or children do have allergies, certain lifestyle strategies—as well as medical options—exist that can make a difference. And some of those strategies, such as getting more fresh air, may not only lessen our allergies but bring with them the promise of many other health-enhancing effects.

Thus Fido or Fluffy may help decrease our allergies after all, which is one more reason to consider sharing your life with a critter.

6. Unrecognized Sources of Wisdom

*Indecency, vulgarity, obscenity—these are strictly confined to man;
he invented them. Among the higher animals there is no trace of them.
They hide nothing. They are not ashamed.*

—Mark Twain (1835 – 1910)

Towering skyscrapers. Traffic jams. Crowded shopping malls. Regardless of whether such imagery brings positive or negative emotions, these descriptions confront us with a stark reality. Most of us live lives far separated from an intimate relationship with our natural environment.

This distancing carries with it benefits as well as liabilities. It's wonderful to live above many of the whims of nature, holed up in a house or apartment with central heat and air conditioning. I'm thankful to be able to hop in a car, board a train, or soar in a plane and cover distances unimaginable to my surefooted or horse-backed predecessors. And how can we but be thankful for indoor plumbing and mechanized devices that save us a trip to the nearest stream or well for such mundane duties as washing ourselves or our clothing?

However, residing in a largely artificial world of electronic gadgets, fast foods, and labor-saving devices has also allowed us—in some respects—to lose sight of ourselves. We know much more about human physiology than did our progenitors, but we often seem to have less insight into how to translate what we know into action. From my vantage point as a physician, it seems that in the midst of all our progress, we have largely lost the ability to sense what our bodies really need and address those concerns. Furthermore, in days filled with largely meaningless activities (such as keeping up with the latest soap opera, TV serial, or sporting event), it is easy to forget to take care of ourselves.

My observations are not unique. Whether you talk about Native Americans, aboriginal Australians, or indigenous peoples of other nations, all saw their health and well being as inextricably connected with nature. Our ancestors knew that ill health was the sure result of losing sight of our connection to the natural world around us.

Over the last several decades, we've seen an increasing crescendo of interest in protecting our environment. This comes as no surprise. We read about fish so contaminated with mercury that they are unsafe to eat, about the broad range of ill health effects linked to air pollution, and about the dangers of water pollution stemming from pesticides and industrial waste. Researchers also warn of the results of the stresses inherent in our artificial, mechanized environments.

This growing realization in many urban settings has resulted in a renewed interest in connecting with nature. This may sound well and good for those with sufficient means to take frequent vacations from their urban surroundings, but how about those who simply cannot afford

frequent forays into nature? Then again, if you live in a large American city—otherwise known as the "concrete jungle"—can even an infrequent weekend trip satisfy the need to reconnect with pleasant fields, mountains, and forests?

Regardless of where we live, pets provide a unique connection with the natural world and in so doing offer a wonderful pathway toward the fulfillment of our deepest longings to return to a simple life. Despite modernization, most of us—either consciously or unconsciously—are becoming aware of our need to find wholeness through connection with the larger world in which we live. This is not just philosophizing on my part. When the National Institutes of Health convened a panel of experts in 1987 to discuss the negative effects of city living and "the rat race," they too suggested that pet ownership "may reflect a largely urban population's often unsatisfied need for intimacy, nurturance, and contact with nature."[20] Dr. Bruce Headey echoed a similar sentiment in a recent editorial, when he stated: "At a fundamental level, the benefits of pets appear linked to the human desire to be close to nature and other living creatures."[21]

Perhaps one of the reasons we are so drawn to our pets is that these companion animals are so simple and unpretentious. They are also in tune with their environment and the needs of their bodies to a much greater degree than we are. There is no question that this ecological awareness can have profound health implications. By watching the good examples of our pets, we can be inspired to change our lifestyle in ways that can enhance our health. Whether it is seeing Fido's pure enjoyment of exercise or listening to the chirping of our parakeets, we can gain valuable insights into our own condition and need for a more simple life.

Today many of the diseases we succumb to are largely the result of our choices. In 1994, Drs. McGinnis and Foege published landmark research that for the first time looked not just at what people ostensibly died from (such as heart disease, cancer, or stroke) but rather at the underlying factors that resulted in their demise.[22] Those factors were largely lifestyle related. The top three causes they identified were: tobacco (claiming approximately 435,000 lives per year), poor diet and activity patterns (leading to the death of 400,000 annually), and alcohol (linked to 85,000 casualties).

Animals, by their lifestyle practices, often speak to us eloquently of what we need to prioritize. Just try to skip Lassie's walk, and she'll let you know your priorities need to be adjusted. Attempt to give your horse some other fluid than water to drink, and you'll get some immediate feedback. These beloved creatures are responding to the needs of their bodies—and the pressures of paying the bills, resolving family arguments, or the latest Wall Street numbers don't impact those drives. We can learn a lesson here.

Our pets also speak to us through their less exemplary characteristics. Now, I know you may be tempted to color your pet's behaviors in the most appealing hues (especially if you often find yourself defending them before non–animal lovers). However, unless you are the fortunate owner of highly exemplary pets who hardly ever mess up—that is, they have never once had an accident on the carpet in front of guests!—then you've had plenty of occasions to observe behaviors unworthy of modeling.

These lapses from perfect behavior don't really undermine the value or overall health benefits of our pets. In fact, I would argue that the faults of our companion animals may be equally as valuable as their good traits—at least when it comes to speaking to us about our own lifestyle.

Think about it for a moment. Do you have any friends who can graciously expose your greatest faults? If you do, do they leave you smiling after the encounter? Such human interactions are rare indeed. However, our pets do this often. We laugh or smile at their faults, only to realize that we're viewing an animal version of some of our own bad habits.

Our pets have the ability to speak to us in ways that no one else can. Consider our two dogs, Bruno and Tuxie. The behavior of Bruno—a male German Shepherd—speaks volumes on the subject of jealousy. There's no question he's top dog when it comes to him and Tuxie (a female Lab-Great Pyrenees mix). However, being king of dogs is not sufficient on the DeRose ranch. Just try to pet Tuxie—or show her any modicum of affection. Bruno will immediately push Tuxie aside and vie for your attention.

Now, I know some animal behaviorists will say that Bruno's behavior is solely driven by canine biological factors. They would take issue with my use of the word *jealousy*. But in the drama that plays out every time we display affection to our dogs, each one who beholds these two is still confronted with solemn questions: Do I ever act the same way? Do I ever feel that I have to be the focus of attention all the time? Does my own human behavior reveal an attitude that says, "Me first!" above the needs of others?

Regardless of the strength of our bond, and regardless of whether I am just a casual observer or an intimate human companion to my pet, Bruno's less-than-exemplary behavior speaks volumes to me. And the behaviors of your pets do the same to you. In their good moments as well as their bad ones, our animals are providing a special window through which we can learn valuable lessons about the importance of unselfish behavior and a better way to live.

This aspect of pets as mirrors into our own characters transcends the normal interpretation of the bond. Yet it is their very capacity to endear themselves to humankind—to bond with us—that causes us to pause long enough to learn from their ways. Furthermore, there is something about animals that inspires the child in all of us. From yesterday's Disney classics to today's Animal Planet channel, from Black Beauty to Bambi, animals have always inspired us with their uncensored affections. When we—like them—interact on a more simple and unguarded, childlike level, the quality of our own lives not only improves, but we even love our pets more. Not only that, but it seems that even our ability to learn from these beloved creatures increases.

To summarize, owning a pet or being around animals may enhance our human health for a variety of reasons:

1. Our pets endear themselves to us, and we can form a relationship or bond with them that has powerful health-promoting effects.

2. Animals instinctively know their own health needs and prioritize them, which can inspire us to address areas we may be tempted to neglect.

3. The faults of our furry friends allow us to look closely at our own deficiencies in a less-threatening way than if pointed out by even our most beloved two-legged companions.

These latter two areas dealing with the example of our animal companions—both good and bad—are worth a careful look. In addition, I have seen in my own life how pets can provide instruction in four other areas (discussed in the next four chapters)—areas that concern the most powerful, natural, health-giving factors that human beings can embrace:

■ Exercise
■ Sunshine
■ Nutrition
■ Social and Spiritual Health

God placed animals on Planet Earth for a reason, and we can learn wonderful lessons if we are only willing to stop long enough to listen intently, observe carefully, and gather wisdom from their examples.

7. Is Exercise Just for the Dogs?

*You can't help someone get up a hill without
getting closer to the top yourself.*
—GENERAL H. NORMAN SCHWARZKOPF

It's time for my walk . . . it's time for my walk," Timmy's bark seems to say. His human companion, Edna, is quite attuned to this appeal. And I have some first-hand knowledge of the subject as well. You see, Edna is both my wife's mother and a periodic resident at the DeRose ranch. When she visits us from her home state of Tennessee, she never comes alone. Timmy, her affectionate dog, always makes the trip with her. None of us know his pedigree, but that cute little guy really knows the importance of exercise. When his walk is overdue, he'll let you know in no uncertain terms.

As we've already observed, most pets have the same knack as Timmy. When it comes to activity, they seem to be in better touch with what their bodies need than we are. It's no surprise—they have fewer distractions. They're not concerned about balancing the checkbook or meeting the yearly demands of the IRS. They are not concerned about how business is doing or whether the Dow Jones average or NASDAQ goes up or down. So why don't we listen to their example?

Let's face it—even if we don't listen to their examples, we listen to their barks. When our pets say it's time to exercise, we generally kick into gear—at least for their sakes—secretly knowing it's also best for us.

Whole treatises have been written on exercise, but it's worth reiterating just how powerful a health-giving agency simple activity is. If you are trying to lower your blood pressure or improve your cholesterol numbers, make sure exercise is on your list. If you are looking for a natural way to boost your mood—or control anxiety—don't forget to move your legs beyond frequent trips to the refrigerator.

Are you afraid of diabetes? Exercise has proven valuable in preventing this modern-day high blood sugar scourge. You can even improve pregnancy outcomes and decrease your risk of certain cancers by regular physical activity. The truth is, proverbial "couch potatoes" do get sick more.

You likely realized that I skipped one of the greatest motivators for regular activity—weight loss. It's true, regular physical activity can help you shed pounds and can also prevent unnecessary weight gain. However, the exercise-weight connection often works to our disadvantage. Look at it this way. If you regularly overindulge in junk food, even a relatively good exercise program may not be sufficient to counteract the girth-augmenting tendencies of your less-than-optimal diet. In this scenario, if weight loss is your main exercise motivator, your resolve can rapidly wane.

Now think about your cat. Tabby doesn't run around her territory in order to fit into a new outfit. She scampers, plays, and hunts because it's part of her nature. She enjoys it, for she was made for action. Honestly, activity is every bit a part of human nature as well. Your whole physiology functions best if you exercise. So don't get overly preoccupied with the bathroom scale. Exercise provides huge benefits even if you don't yet see the downward trajectory of that needle on the scale.

To illustrate, consider the work of researchers at the Cooper Clinic in Dallas. They made some interesting observations about physical fitness and weight that provide a needed perspective. Most Americans wouldn't hesitate if asked to choose between being thin and unfit—or fit and fat. The trim physique would win out (and for many, so much the better if they didn't have to pay the price of exercise).

However, the Cooper researchers found that if you enjoy living, you'd be much better off being fit and overweight than trim and out of shape. At any given age, the men who were fit but fat had only half the risk of death than did their lean, unfit peers.[23] Bottom line: Even if your exercise has not resulted in a super-toned physique, studies such as this one show that you are increasing both the quality and longevity of your life by making fitness a priority.

Yet the news gets even better. Even if your exercise does not seem to be improving your fitness, just being active in itself yields large health dividends. Research consistently reveals that physical activity decreases your risk of heart disease, stroke, and colon cancer.[24] Thus, you not only live longer but can save money in expensive doctor bills.

"OK," you say, "I've got the message. Learn from my horses, listen to my gerbils, follow my fish—and make it a point to keep active."

However, you may also be wondering if engaging in America's most popular pet-related activity—the "walk"—really gives you much in the way of quality exercise. After all, even as your dog is leading you around by his leash, he certainly stops a lot. Contrary to many popular notions, stopping periodically during exercise may actually increase the benefits of the exercise rather than detracting from them. As one of the investigators into intermittent exercise (conducted at Oklahoma's Lifestyle Center of America), I can tell you that we found people lost more weight and experienced a greater decrease in body fat if they incorporated short periods of rest into their exercise routine. This concept of "intermittent training"—or stopping and starting—is growing in popularity. Depending on the regimen, it may also help improve performance, enhance thyroid function, and decrease the risk of injury.

How do you go about doing "intermittent exercise?" One way is to take your dog for a walk and stop when she wants to stop. If you want a more scientific approach, get with an exercise physiologist or physician. He or she can determine your target heart range with a treadmill test. Once that range has been determined (say, for example, it's 100 to 110 beats per minute), you're ready to exercise. Using a heart rate monitor, exercise until you reach 110 (the upper limit of your ten-beat target range). Then stop your vigorous activity and "rest" by engaging in a cool-down type of exercise (such as moving your feet in place while Duchess is sniffing the fire hydrant). When your heart rate drops to 100 (the lower limit of your ten-beat range), go back to your more vigorous activity (apologize to your dog, and tell her it's time to go).

When an unfit person starts on such a regimen, she may be exercising for only about thirty seconds and then resting for thirty seconds. As she gets more fit, however, the amount of rest time will decrease relative to the amount of time spent in actual exercise.

What happens if you don't have time to get in your thirty minutes per day of exercise? Listen to your pets. Just let the average indoor cat get near an open door, and see what happens. If he has a chance to bolt outside, he will—even if it's only for a few minutes. Take this message to heart. We now know that you can measurably improve your immune system with as little as five minutes of moderate exercise. Beside that, the benefits of exercise are cumulative. Five minutes now, ten minutes later, and before you know it, you've put in a half hour for the day. For many of the benefits of exercise—thirty minutes spread out over the day is as beneficial as a single thirty-minute session.

As in other areas, when it comes to exercise, we should take special note of the good example our pets set for us. However, if you have an animal that likes more human pursuits, such as lying around watching TV, realize that he's become too "humanized" and, from his negative example, draw motivation to change. Either way, make a point to get some type of regular physical exercise. It's best to do something six or seven days a week. Even though I'm a big advocate of having at least one rest day per week, on that day I don't recommend just lying around with your feet up. I still put physical activity on the list. But we're talking just a leisurely walk or a pleasant bicycle ride—not a seventh day of training.

An ancient Chinese proverb says, "The journey of a thousand miles begins with the first step." How true. So follow the lead of your dog, grab that leash, and begin the trip.

Believe me, all the scientific research says your body will thank you.

More Readers Respond . . .
. . . to *Will My Pet Go to Heaven?*

Dear Steve, Little did we know when we bought your book and read it that in less than two weeks we would need the comfort it gives. [The story of Scruffy is told]. Your book had proved invaluable to us during this time of crisis and grief. I am going to order more tomorrow. We want to give one to each of the vets. They suffered right along with us. We believe that your book will be beneficial to them and will help them in ministering to others when they lose a pet. We are also going to give one to our neighbors across the street. I know that your book will be a blessing to them as well. Thank you for writing a sensitive, biblical book about pets and heaven. May the Lord richly bless you. My wife and our three rescued (all were strays) canine children thank you as well.

George T. Washburn, Th.D.

Marion, Alabama

Hi Steve, My name is Kathrin. I just wanted to write and let you know that I really enjoyed reading your book *Will My Pet Go to Heaven?* A lady in my church gave it to me for Christmas. I was glad to read a book on the subject because I've always had questions about that. I have LOTS of animals. Right now one of our family cats is sitting here with me at the computer. Anyways, I have had lots of animals die in the past, and I know how hard it is. Thanks for writing a book on this.

God bless you,

Kathrin Ashby

8. Let the Sun Shine In

Keep your face to the sunshine and you cannot see the shadow.
—HELEN KELLER (1880 – 1968)

It's a cool, early spring afternoon in Oklahoma. Yesterday's gusty winds are past, and the sun beams down through a cloudless sky. It doesn't take too many guesses to figure out where the animals are at the DeRose place. You're sure to find them all enjoying the sunshine in some way. Our quarter horse and pony are grazing in one part of the pasture. The goats have taken a temporary break from a similar routine and are now basking in the sun. Gracie and Buttons, our cats, are outside stalking grasshoppers in the green grass. Bruno and Tuxie are playing their dog games in the sun.

We all know that reptiles need that warmth to raise their metabolism and increase their efficiency for protecting themselves, hunting, mating, or whatever the day's activities may hold. But why does the sun on a cool day hold such attraction for the mammals who call our place home?

Keeping warm and enjoying the sun's radiant heat may be the immediate motivators for animals. However, sunshine is actually just as vital to their health as it is to ours. Like humans, many of our pets require sunshine to make vitamin D—an important vitamin-hormone. Grazing animals such as cows and horses can make this essential vitamin on their own, so long as they're getting adequate sunlight, but carnivores such as dogs and cats don't have this capacity. Instead, they must get it by eating prey that has produced its own vitamin D. In civilized society, our cats and dogs get the vitamin in their animal chow.

How important is the "Big D" anyway, and what does it do? First of all—as most of us may vaguely know—it plays an important role in bone health. However, medical scientists are beginning to appreciate many additional far-reaching benefits of this vital nutrient. For example, vitamin D also has beneficial effects on the immune system. Over twenty years ago, researchers were struck by the higher colon cancer rates in the northern states as compared to the sunbelt. As the data came together, insufficient vitamin D levels in the north appeared to provide the explanation. Vitamin D also appears to have a protective effect against prostate, breast, and ovarian cancers.

The immune-augmenting effects of vitamin D go beyond discussions of cancer. It appears that this vitamin also aids in decreasing our risk of a host of autoimmune diseases—conditions where the body's immune system literally attacks itself. Take, for example, multiple sclerosis (MS). This potentially debilitating nervous system disorder occurs as the body destroys myelin, a nerve-fiber insulating material. Scientist have now linked an increased risk of MS to insufficient blood levels of vitamin D. Type 1 diabetes, an autoimmune condition formerly called juvenile-

31

onset diabetes, also shows a link to vitamin D levels. In Finland, where sunlight is a very scarce wintertime commodity, low vitamin D levels have been linked to the development of diabetes in infants.

Even when it comes to bone health, most Americans fail to recognize the range of symptoms that can be linked to vitamin D. For example, vitamin D deficiency contributes to more than osteoporosis. Insufficiencies of this vitamin lie at the root of *osteomalacia*—a condition which can cause bone pain coupled with muscle aches and weakness. These symptoms may be mistaken for fibromyalgia. Consequently, anyone with a fibromyalgia diagnosis should be carefully evaluated for their level of vitamin D.

However, sunshine provides more than vitamin D. It naturally lifts our mood, in part by boosting levels of melatonin—a hormone that helps support restorative sleep. This is why, with shorter, fewer sun-filled winter days, people face an increased risk of the depressive syndrome known as *seasonal affective disorder* (SAD). Ultraviolet light exposure, as provided by the sun, has also been documented to lower blood pressure. This effect may be partially mediated by vitamin D, but it may also involve sunshine-induced relaxation.

Further adding to the importance of sunshine is its primacy among vitamin D sources. Clearly, humans appear designed to get this vitamin from the sun rather than from food. Vitamin D is thus unlike every other vitamin, in that we are not dependent for it on a dietary source. However, if you live in the northern half of the United States, you likely face a vitamin D deficit in the winter months. Getting outside a lot during those months is unlikely to boost your vitamin D levels sufficiently, because during those shorter days, the sun's ultraviolet rays are not intense enough to boost vitamin D production by your skin.

Surprisingly, even in the summer, more and more Americans are coming up vitamin D-deficient. Forty-two percent of a representative sample of African-American women, aged 15 to 49 years old, were recently reported to be vitamin D deficient.[25] Among healthy male and female Bostonians between 18 and 29 years old, 36 percent lacked adequate levels of vitamin D.[26]

The culprit? A lack of time spent outdoors—owing to increased hours spent in sedentary indoor pursuits such as computer gaming and TV viewing. Other factors further compromise vitamin D production. More darkly pigmented individuals, older Americans, and the obese all have a harder time making vitamin D. However, perhaps our greatest problem lies with our national preoccupation with skin cancer prevention. Slap some sunscreen on (even if it is a low SPF number such as 8) and you'll make virtually no vitamin D. One alternative is to get exposed to some rays first before using sun-protective agents. After fifteen or twenty minutes, go ahead then and apply your sunscreen.

Relatively few dietary sources of vitamin D exist. If you regularly take fish oil or eat fatty fish (such as salmon) three to four times weekly, you may already be eating enough vitamin D. However, few Americans fall into this category. Fortunately, milk is routinely supplemented with vitamin D. Orange juice can also be fortified with this vitamin.

Other than convenience, there is no significant advantage to getting your vitamin D in milk or juice as compared to taking a vitamin D pill. Vitamin D expert Michael Holick, M.D., of Boston University, is a strong proponent of sun exposure to maximize levels of this critical vitamin. However, in areas far from the equator, he encourages 800 to 1000 I.U. of vitamin D daily during the winter months.

When it comes to the importance of vitamin D, it is fortunate that most of our pets can't read the latest scientific reports. If they did, they would be liable to fall into the trap we humans often stumble into. Namely, if a little is good, more must be better. In the case of Vitamin D, this logic can be dangerous and even fatal. In high doses, vitamin D is extremely toxic—both to humans as well as to animals. Ensure that your pets get adequate sunshine, or provide a ready source of vitamin D in species that can't make their own. (Fortunately, dog and cat foods are fortified with this necessary nutrient.)

Veterinarians report particular problems with overzealous pet owners overdosing their birds and reptiles on this vitamin. Excessive doses can result in calcification of these creatures' kidneys and stomachs. And we're not talking about massive overdoses—three to four times their actual need will often put them into a death spiral.

Once again, we can learn from our animals how important sunshine is to the human organism, and most of us would do well to imitate their preference for outdoor activity. In the beginning of the world, God said, "Let there be light" (Genesis 1:3, 16), and He provided the sun as our main source for its healing rays. Sunshine tends to boost your mood as well as your vitamin D levels. If skin cancer concerns loom large in your mind, opt for 800 -1000 I.U. of vitamin D daily. Whether from the blazing orb in the sky, a pill, or through fortified food, make sure you get the benefits your body needs.

Pull back the shades too. Sunlight may fade your couch, but it could save your life.

9. Taking Counsel From Cats

I have studied many philosophers and many cats.
The wisdom of cats is infinitely superior.
—HIPPOLYTE TAINE (1828 – 1898)

Other than choosing whether or not to smoke, your eating habits are the single most powerful lifestyle influence affecting your quality of life and longevity. Diet is not only about *what* you eat—it also includes *how* we eat.

When it comes to eating, our two dogs, Bruno and Tuxie, are as different as night and day. Bruno, a trim German Shepherd, is a gregarious five-year-old. By now you've probably gathered that his highest priority is to be with any two-legged family member who is present. For Bruno, eating is only a necessary task.

Tuxie, our Labrador Retriever–Great Pyrenees mix, is several years Bruno's senior. She once seemed to share Bruno's pragmatic outlook on food. However, part of the deal when we acquired her from the animal shelter was that we would have her neutered. Ever since that fateful surgery, Tuxie's greatest object in life has been to eat. More than once, she's managed to get into a cache of dog food. In her record gourmand accomplishment, she put away an estimated fifteen pounds of dog food in a mere two hours. We found her looking as if she were ready to deliver a litter—but totally content.

The only way to feed Bruno is to make sure there is no chance for Tuxie to access his food. Bruno will take his time, reveling in the human companionship. On the other hand, when food is placed in Tuxie's dish, it will stay there only a matter of seconds. She virtually inhales her entire meal.

Bruno and Tuxie pay eloquent testimony to two differing eating styles popular among humans. As with Bruno, we are endowed early in life with a distaste for overeating. Just try to get a newborn to overeat. It's impossible. She will spit out her food, or he will turn his head away—baby is done, and that's all there is to it.

However, most of us learn to be like Tuxie. We gobble our food down, looking for more sensory enjoyment even if we don't need the nutrition. It's hard to hear a doctor tell us that we need to lose weight. Even less comforting is realizing that our "friends" are speaking behind our back about our bulging girth. Gazing at Tuxie's eating habits confronts us with reality and the probing question: Am I really *that* fixated on food?

On the other hand, our two cats, Gracie and Buttons, are models when it comes to standing above the level of peer influences. These two newer additions to our menagerie came with the promise of keeping down the rodent population in our barn. There was no question regarding our motivation—at least in part—for wanting to adopt them into the family. However, knowing cats, do you think either one of them obediently yielded to our expectations for catching mice or other rodents?

Day by day, they play out their hunting preferences. They say in effect, "Birds? Of course. Insects? Why not? But mice? You've got to be kidding!" Granted, we probably made mistakes early on by making our intentions too apparent to this traditionally independent species. It was probably unwise to bring both Gracie and Buttons face to face with field mice that we'd occasionally corner after lifting a log or stirring up a pile of brush. Making our aspirations for our cats so overtly known no doubt put our felines in an unenviable position. As much as they might display affection for us, they couldn't damage their reputations for being highly self-willed, spirited creatures and still acquiesce to our wishes.

However, our two cats—and the feline species in general—are enviable role models when it comes to diet. We have been so habituated to eating for social reasons that we often allow the choices of those around us to sabotage our best intentions. We eat when we're not hungry. We eat food that aggravates our diabetes or high blood pressure or cholesterol problems. We even make dietary decisions that perpetuate that ongoing battle with our weight. Why do we do it? Partly because we have not listened carefully enough to our cats. Cats rise above their peer influences. It doesn't matter if the head of the household will be offended because they didn't eat what was on the menu. They chart their own course, stick with it, and do what they know to be right for them, no matter what we humans dictate.

We should all take counsel from cats. By this I mean that we should eat what *we* decide is best for us—on *our* terms. Not that we shouldn't care for the feelings of others or enjoy the company of friends and family. But at the same time—while maintaining sensitivity to the feelings of those around us and encouraging social interaction—we must chart our own undeviating dietary course.

St. Louis University physicians John E. Morley and David Thomas sent out a stunning press release in March 2002. In it, they pinpointed an often-unrecognized malady that insidiously kills—or contributes to the death of—literally millions of older Americans. The culprit? Loss of appetite.

As the girth of Americans continues to swell, losing one's appetite may sound more fortuitous than dangerous. However, appetite loss—particular in older adults—may be the beginning of a spiral that ends in the grave. Malnutrition depresses the body's immune system and puts an individual at high risk for succumbing to infectious illness. Although deliberately shedding unwanted pounds can be desirable if it occurs through a healthier diet or more exercise, inadvertent weight loss can be a veritable death sentence.

It's no exaggeration to speak of millions being affected. Consider a recent study from the University of Guelph in Canada.[27] There, researchers Keller and McKenzie attempted to uncover nutritional risk factors in a sample of community-living seniors. They looked for eating patterns that put individuals at risk for health problems down the road. Keller and McKenzie found what they were looking for, documenting patterns of significant nutritional risk in 68.7 percent of those evaluated. Even more startling, 44.4 percent were at high nutritional risk. Poor appetite was among the leading factors contributing to elevated risk of future problems. Other key factors included poor food intake and difficulties chewing, cooking, or shopping for food.

How can someone know if appetite is precariously ebbing away? On behalf of the Council for Nutritional Clinical Strategies in Long-Term Care, Drs. Morley and Thomas unveiled a tool designed to spot danger signals of a poor appetite. Their eight-question, multiple-choice survey really centers on six different warning signs of a dangerously failing desire for food.

The following six questions get at these issues more simply than the council's survey—providing you with some framework to evaluate the key issues. Answer these questions yourself, then share them with any older adults you know. The more questions to which you answer "Yes," the more likely it is that your appetite is dangerously eroding, exposing you to potential adverse health effects:

1. Is real hunger unusual for you—even at meal times?
2. Do you often feel full after eating relatively little?
3. Does food taste significantly worse now than it did earlier in your life?
4. Is it common for you to get nauseated when you eat?
5. Have you inadvertently decreased the number of times you eat in a day?
6. Do you frequently feel sad or depressed?

How did you score? Realize that answering "Yes" to even one question is a warning sign. Therefore, if you haven't already done so, bring any positive responses to the attention of a health professional. That's something best done sooner than later. Many of the symptoms reflected by those six simple questions can indicate an underlying depression. Prompt treatment can often help you make a rapid recovery. However, failing appetite can be a sign of other problems as well. A good diagnosis goes a long way toward finding the proper therapy. So find out why your appetite is failing. And be aware that the solution may be more pleasant than you imagined.

This is where pets come front and center into our dialogue. The really good news about appetite problems is that these beloved animals may actually hold the key to turning your situation around. (But before you diagnose yourself as just needing a little more animal therapy—make sure a health professional also concurs with your assessment.)

How is it that the key to your appetite problems may be wagging its tail under your table or purring on your lap at this very moment? In the DeRose household, our pets—particularly our dogs—have taught us some principles of appetite maintenance. Spending time with some of your animals will likely convince you of the same.

I remember one of the fringe benefits of marrying my wife, Sonja. In addition to all her other good qualities, I got to share more intimately in the life of Jacer, her German Shepherd. Jacer was a tremendous dog—*the standard* by which all our other dogs have been compared. Yet that noble German Shepherd always made it clear that eating was a social time. He politely but unmistakably indicated that it was our responsibility to stay with him while he ate.

This powerful lesson is one that it would be well for single Americans to take to heart. Especially in our later years when we may outlive many life companions and friends, our pets remind us that eating is a social time. Your pets may supply some of that social need. They may also inspire you to make contact with other humans a priority when it comes to meal times. Either way, you're likely to find an increase in appetite by getting out of the rut of eating alone.

Scientists have now "proven" what Jacer and his relatives have known for centuries: When someone eats with you, you tend to eat more. If you are taking food to an older person—whether as part of a structured program or just out of concern—don't just leave the food and run. Stick around. If you could measure the results, odds are that the person will eat much more with you there.

There is another way that animals can help address the problem of waning hunger sensations that tend to plague our later years. They can remind us of the need for variety. I've already pointed out that our current German Shepherd, Bruno, is a much more finicky eater than Tuxie. Whereas Tuxie will gladly accept just about anything off our table, Bruno isn't typically enamored with our preferred vegetarian fare. He clearly desires "real" dog food. But he too, lets us know that he's not just going to polish off one of those fifty-pound bags before we need to open another one. He wants a fairly regular rotation of his menu if we expect him to eat well.

Variety is another key part of the formula for better eating later in life. Don't make a large dish and then expect to eat some of it each night as you dine alone in quiet desperation. Have something different every day. This will also go a long way toward maintaining or improving your appetite.

Right eating habits are important. However, it goes without saying that what we eat also has a powerful bearing on our health. Diet books are always big sellers, and depending on the era and on whom you interview, you'll likely come up with very different answers as to optimal food choices. Over the course of my twenty years as a physician, I've seen diet gurus come and go. I've listened to the latest theories, only to find them fall out of vogue. However, one thing has been a constant—if we would eat more like our pets, we would have better health.

Some may immediately take this as strong advocacy for the Atkins diet or other low-carb eating styles. Yes, that would be a reasonable conclusion if we were like our dogs or our cats. However, it would not be a safe deduction if you're comparing yourself to a horse or a goat.

The bottom line is that, left to their own devices, animal eat in a way that is most consistent with their unique physiology. Some years ago, one of America's most prolific research cardiologists, Dr. William Roberts, looked at this very question. He studied the tooth structure of humans—he noticed it was best suited to grind and chew things like nuts, seeds, grains, fruits, and vegetables. Our teeth were not well equipped to tear flesh. Roberts made similar observations with respect to the length of our digestive tract (long like a plant eater, as opposed to short like a carnivore) and our hands (lacking claws or other sharp structures as found in flesh eaters) as well as other aspects of human anatomy and physiology. He concluded: "Humans are not carnivores."[28]

Therefore, if we were really to listen to the example of our animal friends, we would be at least semi-vegetarians—if not eschewing all forms of flesh. Granted, even mentioning the word *vegetarian* in a book dealing with pets is not likely to evoke neutral emotions. You may relate intimately to militant vegetarians—or you may simply have personally chosen to forgo flesh for ethical or humane reasons. On the other hand, you may become livid when you sense that activists are bent on depriving us of some of the very national foods we were raised on. After all, what would a Fourth of July barbecue be without hot dogs and burgers—or Thanksgiving without turkey, or New Year's without ham?

However, many find that as they get closer to their pets, it becomes harder to think about eating their cousins. Just ask any farm kid: It's typically pretty tough to eat an animal that you've bonded with as a pet.

I haven't even mentioned the health benefits of eating more fruits and vegetables. But then, your mother and both your grandmothers likely told you as much. Suffice it to say that medical research continues to confirm the health wisdom of loading up on more fruits, vegetables, nuts, seeds, and grains. Make sure the latter category features the "whole grains" such as whole wheat, unrefined brown rice, or rolled oats. Whole grains, along with other plant products, provide you with a liberal supply of fiber and a powerful complement of *phytochemicals* (plant nutrients). This blend is calculated to lower your cholesterol, decrease your risk of cancer, improve or prevent your diabetes, and help you shed unwanted pounds.

This all should come as no surprise. When mom and grandma and your pets all agree, how could science say otherwise?

10. Social and Spiritual Health

He behaved throughout with decent fortitude,
equanimity and self-possession.[29]

—CHARLES DICKENS, DESCRIBING THE FATAL ILLNESS OF HIS PET RAVEN, "GRIP"

Rita could never quite figure out her mother, Geraldine. At 80 years of age, Geraldine was in good health, but it had become impossible to get her to go on any extended trips. Leaving her home for any length of time was virtually out of the question. The issue always centered on care for Midnight, her Siamese cat.

"What's the big deal?" thought Rita. Other family members lived just a few blocks away—as well as neighbors residing even closer—any one of whom would be happy to look out for Midnight. After all, it didn't require much effort to care for a cat that freely roamed the country environs around Geraldine's house all day. Putting food in her bowl once a day was all that was needed to care for the cat (the creek beside the house eliminated any concerns about dehydration). When Rita pointed out the ease of the cat care, all her mother would say is, "I don't want to be a burden on any of those overworked people."

After many frustrating conversations, it finally dawned on Rita. Her good-natured and compassionate mother was not primarily concerned about unduly burdening her neighbors or other family members. This was just an excuse (consciously or subconsciously formulated) that seemed less selfish than the real reason for her hesitancy to travel: Her mother couldn't stand being apart from her beloved pet. Once Rita recognized the real dynamics, she immediately came up with a solution: Midnight would travel with them as part of the family. Geraldine had no more difficulty when it came to taking long trips.

Although we may be tempted to feel self-conscious about our affection for our pets, we shouldn't. There's nothing wrong with these tender ties—provided we don't allow undue affection for our pets to undermine important human relationships. As we saw in a previous chapter, many doctors are finding that the social bond that exists between a pet and its human companion is a powerfully positive, health-giving force.

But animals provide more than companionship, blood-pressure benefits, or dietary insights. They are also powerful mentors when it comes to learning about the social and spiritual dimensions of life. This is an immense topic, but five examples of their teaching skills seem especially apropos:

1. Selfless service

2. Tolerance of mistakes

3. A reason for living

4. Loyalty

5. Rest and contentment

Selfless Service

Turning on lights and opening doors are just a few of the tasks that Liberty, a Golden Retriever, performs for her wheelchair-bound companion, Mavis. Mavis's service dog has truly provided her with more than companionship. The single 57-year-old now can get through a day with considerably greater ease. Liberty has made her multiple sclerosis limitations much less daunting.

What motivates Liberty and other service dogs? It is simply the satisfaction of a job well done and the appreciation that comes from the recipients of their kindness. What a noble example for us humans to follow!

Mark Finley, of television's *It Is Written,* tells the story of how a man wanted to take a long trip with his dog. In order to prepare for his journey, he inquired in advance as to whether his pet would be welcome at various establishments. One hotel manager wrote him a letter that went something like this:

"I have never had a dog stay in my hotel…that stole any of my towels, pilfered my sheets, walked off with the pictures, or caused a drunken disturbance…. By all means bring your dog, and if he recommends you, you can stay too."

Our companion animals can be selfless servants in other ways as well. Because of their size, habits of life, or other physiologic or behavioral factors, our pets often place themselves in harm's way without even realizing it. Such is the case when it comes to poisoning. The annals of medical history record examples of how pets contributed to the health of their human companions by serving as "sentinels" of toxic problems.

For example, on a number of occasions, lead poisoning has been identified in children as a result of first diagnosing pets with the condition.[30] This is an important contribution. Lead poisoning often goes undetected in children. It can cause no symptoms, yet have significant and lasting adverse mental health effects. Therefore, pets sometimes are the heralds of serious problems in a home—not by their barks or their whimpers but rather by providing early evidence of exposure in their own bodies, which can be detected by the skilled analysis of the family veterinarian.

Tolerance of Mistakes

Even when our pets behave poorly, our affection for them often inspires us to find solutions, rather than abandoning them. Veterinary experts know that animal behavior problems often have to do with less-than-ideal situations in the physical environment in which they live. Dr. Shirley Seaman, of Edinburgh University's Royal School of Veterinary Studies, has gone on record: "The behavior of companion animals is affected by the environment in which they are kept . . . this can lead to the development of behavioral problems."[31]

These are extremely important issues. When we understand that there are reasons for our pets' bad behaviors, we can constructively address them. In fact, most pet owners start with the premise that their pet is basically good—and just has some bad characteristics that can be addressed by better training or the improvement of circumstances.

If we could carry this lesson over into our human relations, this would go a long way in helping us be more compassionate toward those who exhibit behavioral problems. The problems we see in animals—followed by solutions that work—teach us to view human beings with kindness and to see them as individuals who more often than not would like to improve, if only their circumstances were changed. This knowledge motivates us to seek to better understand their difficulties, address the causes of their mistakes, and then to improve their situations as an aid to promoting healthy, long-term relationships. In other words, if you make a dog's life easier, he'll be happier and nicer to live with. It's the same with humans.

A Reason for Living

Denise Wood, a lecturer at the University of South Australia and a real nature lover, found her dream house several years ago. Although a one-hour commute away from her job, the five-acre farm provided both privacy and a place to live with her diverse assortment of pets that included alpacas, kangaroos, and wallabies. The farm, an old piece of mining property that was worked back in the late 1800s, also gave Denise a place to care for both her regular pets and other animal "castaways."

One summer day, Denise had just finished caring for her latest charge—an infant possum whose mother had recently been struck and killed by a car. She then went out to tend to her alpacas. In the course of her duties, she noticed a small hole. Wondering if a burrowing rodent had made it, she went over to explore. However, when Denise got within several feet of the hole, the ground gave way. She went plunging down a one-hundred-foot mineshaft and landed in cold, dingy water. Miraculously, she survived not only the fall but also nearly forty-eight hours—much of it treading water—in the cold, dark pit.

It seemed that two things kept her going through that ordeal: her faith in a God who heard her prayers, and a sense of purpose based on her knowledge that many of her above-ground pets were dependent on her for survival. In her water-filled tomb, she prayed, "Lord, I know You gave me these animals to look after. Please save *me* so I can save *them!*"[32]

Yes, relationships with animals not only bring us joy and happiness—emotions which can improve our health[32, 33]—but the knowledge that our animals are dependent on us also increases our reasons for living. Most animals are not like bumps on a log but are intensely purposeful creatures. As we develop friendships with them, they add additional purpose to our own lives as well.

Loyalty

Over a century and a half ago in Edinburgh, Scotland, a small Kyleakin Skye Terrier named

Bobby walked the beat with his policeman-companion, John Grey. Tragedy struck the inseparable team in 1858, when John died. Yet even death did not quench Bobby's devotion. He faithfully followed the funeral procession to Grayfriar's churchyard, where John was interred. Although the mourners made their way home, Bobby stayed at the gravesite—faithfully watching over his master.

For years the routine continued—regardless of cold or wind, rain or snow. A kindly cemetery caretaker would, with difficulty, coax Bobby into a place of shelter during the worst weather. Other kindly townspeople made sure the dog was fed regularly. The undying devotion of Grayfriar's Bobby epitomizes the quality of bonding so often characteristic of our beloved pets. Indeed, animals often bestow a lifelong gift of loyalty on their human companions. Such loyalty is an admirable example to us in our service to God and man.

Rest and Contentment

We've all heard the expression, "It's a dog's life." What is a dog's life really like? One of the things we seem to envy in our animals is their ability to take guiltless rest. They can lie down any time, day or night, and without the smallest pang of conscience.

Maybe it's time we listen to them. Truly, it doesn't take much to make your dog or cat happy. Do their carefree lifestyles have something to teach us about cultivating contentment with the simple pleasures of life and about taking time to do what is most important? I think so.

There was a time in my life when to admit my need for sleep seemed less than manly. I was more macho if I could perform well on fewer hours of sleep. When much younger and extremely foolish, I even tried to convince myself that a need for sleep was only a figment of my imagination.

Yes, I could accomplish a lot on little sleep, but my higher powers of intellect suffered. My creativity was not optimal. And I would find myself dozing if I took time for meditation, prayer, or reflection. In our overachieving age, we often short ourselves on sleep and pay for it in increased auto accidents, higher rates of heart attacks, and shorter tempers.

Animals teach us the profound message of resting well with what we have—contentment with the ways things are. Looked at from another perspective, our companion animals teach us the value of living in the present. They tell us to slow down and focus on relationships and the things that make live worth living.

In October of 2000, the *Reader's Digest* featured an article called "The Tomorrow Trap" that likely touched an answering chord with thousands of Americans. Two such readers wrote in and had their letters published on page 14 of the December 2000 issue.

Marie Lieurance of Zillah, Washington, described a sobering incident in her work at a small hospital. She recounted how the tragedy of holding a dying three-year-old in her arms provided a wake up call for her—and her family—to live in the present, because tomorrow never comes for some of us.

A health crisis helped Diane Schoelles or Moreno Valley, California, step off a whirlwind schedule that included being wife, mother, student, and financial analyst at a prestigious company. Only after being forced by her health to "retire" at age 42 could she say, "My children and husband are happy, and my attitude is changing toward living [in] the here and now—rather than in the then and maybe."

Yes, animals teach us to live in the present. We can live whirlwind lives, but there is no way to give a dog a ten-second walk or to groom a horse in twenty-two seconds. Animals often cause us to slow down—and for the many of us who do not know how to do so, they are a boon, indeed.

11. A Lesson From the Peacock

He who never sacrificed a present to a future good or a personal to a general one can speak of happiness only as the blind do of colors.
—OLYMPIA BROWN, 1835-1926, AMERICAN WOMEN'S SUFFRAGE LEADER

"Mommy, Mommy—the peacock is in our yard, and I think it's hurt!" blurted 12-year-old Heather Jones as she came rushing into the house. In most households, that would have sounded like a shocking declaration. However, Alice Jones and her children had noticed the stray peacock wandering on their rural Arkansas property for the last three weeks. So although her child's words prompted concern for the peacock's welfare, the presence of the bird was no surprise.

When Alice reached the bird, Heather's assessment was obviously correct. The peacock was hopping on one leg as his second leg dangled uselessly. Despite his injury, the bird was not at all interested in the attempts of a mother and daughter to catch him (in preparation for a friendly medical evaluation, of course). The peacock was still well able to fly, so with several flaps of his wings, he safely positioned himself in a large oak tree twenty or thirty feet from the ground.

At this point Heather summoned her 9-year-old brother Craig. Craig took a long stick and climbed up a cedar tree beside the peacock's temporary oak retreat. Using the stick to gently nudge the bird, Craig enticed the peacock to fly back to the ground. Instantly, mother and sister again gave chase. Mr. Peacock then made a grave mistake. He tried to hide under some bushes. Alice and her children surrounded the bird. With the assistance of an old piece of heavy material, Alice finally caught the majestic creature.

Heather and Craig were delighted with their new pet. However, Mr. Peacock was clearly unenthusiastic with his new home. He was cooped up in a large dog cage, which did not seem—to him at least—to be the best medicine for his ailments. There was little room to move, and he seemed unable to fathom the benefits. Obviously, Mr. Peacock clearly longed to be outside, enjoying God's nature. Yet unknown to him, his captivity was designed for his own benefit. For a while, he was kept from enjoying the fresh air and open sky, but in time, after his leg healed, he would ultimately once again be able to savor the freedom granted by his Creator.

This true story reminds me about the importance of sacrificing things now for future benefits. Sometimes we need to give up things we want to do and even experience what we consider to be a confinement of our freedom. But if we are sacrificing for God, for the good of others, or for our own higher good, the results will pay off in the long run. Someday, according to the Good Book, there will indeed come once again a heaven on earth, which will include unparalleled enjoyment for all of God's creatures—both human and animal—throughout the ceaseless ages of eternity. We read that . . .

Wolves and sheep will live together in peace,
and leopards will lie down with young goats.
Calves and lion cubs will feed together,
and little children will take care of them.
Cows and bears will eat together,
and their calves and cubs will lie down in peace.
Lions will eat straw as cattle do.
Even a baby will not be harmed
if it plays near a poisonous snake.
On Zion, God's sacred hill,
there will be nothing harmful or evil.
The land will be as full of knowledge
of the Lord as the seas are full of water.

—ADAPTED FROM ISAIAH 11:6-9

For some human beings, despite the many benefits available from animal companions, owning a pet may not be in a person's best interest. In a world marred by sin, even the presence of friendly animals does not always bring comfort. For those with compromised immune systems, some pets—especially birds and reptiles—may not be in one's best interest and sometimes can even be particularly dangerous. Severe allergies can also keep even the most avid cat lover away from the feline objects of his desire.

Sometimes, just like the peacock that had to be restricted for its own good, we have to suffer the loss of something good for the promise of something better. But don't worry. That "something better" will surely come to this suffering planet we call home (see the next section of this book).

For those who have chosen to appreciate the loving ways of their Creator, the sacrifice will be well worth the price.

12. Millions Do Wonder

So far this book has focused on the benefits animals can bring to us in this life, but what about the afterlife? Is it possible that the special friendships we've developed in this world might continue "on the other side"? Believe it or not, millions of animal-loving human beings have asked themselves at one time or another, *Will my pet go to heaven?* I don't think this is an exaggeration because, first of all, this very question often pops into The Question Box during my Bible prophecy seminars. Second, a Christian woman who regularly gives home Bible studies to people on various topics told me once, "This is one of the most common questions I get!"

Beyond this, based on the numerous pre-press comments I've received from both friends and

strangers, I realize that many are extremely interested in my search for an answer to this question. A tall red-headed woman once asked me, "When will your pet book be finished? I know seven people who want to read it!" I talked to a stranger at the Dallas airport in the line by the ticket counter; as she clutched her own four-legged friend, she said earnestly, "I'll buy it!"

Later that same day a man sat down beside me as we waited for our rides from the Oklahoma City airport. With time to kill, I had just booted up my computer laptop to work on this manuscript. "I'm writing a book," I commented, as we began a friendly visit. "About what?" he asked with interest. I told him, and before we parted, he said eagerly, "I'd like to read that book!" I could go on and on. Truly, this subject strikes a common chord in many hearts. The reason is simple: People really love their animals.

The love for a horse is just as complicated as the love for another human being. . . . If you have never loved a horse, you will never understand.
—AUTHOR UNKNOWN

During this short life of ours it's easy to become attached to one of God's more intelligent, non-human creatures, be it a dog, a cat, a bird, a horse, or some other friendly companion. Dogs aren't called "Man's Best Friend" for nothing. For those that have them, pets truly become part of the family. They live, sleep, eat, play, cry, lick, cuddle, and prance around in and outside our homes. People build them their own little houses, buy them special treats, put funny clothes on them, take them on trips, check them into pet-friendly hotels, reserve spaces for them on airlines, watch them give birth to babies, take them to pet doctors when they're sick, pay big money for pet insurance, agonize as they go through major surgeries, and even include them in their wills and estate planning.

Many animals are quite smart, too. When they sense we're hurt, they do their furry best to bring comfort. In not a few cases—as we saw earlier in this book—pets have both risked their lives in incredibly heroic efforts to save their owners. Dramatic tales involving these super-animals are often reported on the popular TV show, "Miracle Pets," or on the Animal Planet channel. Some of these pets have even been awarded medals of honor.

Some of my best leading men have been dogs and horses.
—ELIZABETH TAYLOR (B. 1932)

Not surprisingly, when these almost-human companions breathe their last breaths, their deaths can cause the deepest pain. Many grief-stricken owners bury their animals under pet tombstones in pet cemeteries—cemeteries which are springing up around the world and offer a full line of cremation and burial services. After the heartbreaking funerals, animal graves are visited just as are human graves. Pet photos are cherished just as are pictures of parents, children, grandparents, brothers, and sisters. Many grieving humans turn to professional counselors who offer a variety of pet bereavement resources and support groups. And with the growth of twenty-first century techno-wizardry, more and more pet owners are considering the possibility of cloning their departed pet.

What should a parent say to a teary-eyed child who asks, after the family dog, cat, or horse dies, "Will Rover, Snow Ball, or Black Beauty be in heaven?" Answers such as, "Of course, sweetheart," or, "Rover went to doggie heaven," are typical. But let's be serious. Are such re-

sponses simply fairy-tale talk as unreal as Santa Claus? Or is it possible that a heartbroken boy or girl (not to mention parent) might really see Rover, Snow Ball, or Black Beauty again?

This section of this book is not about fairy tales, fiction, or fantasies such as E.T., Star Wars, Jurassic Park, Lion King, Shrek, or Lord of the Rings. Instead, it's about a heart-felt question, the Holy Bible, and the truth. Ever since I first began my spiritual quest, God has become very real to me, and He has proven His love many times. After studying the Bible for twenty-plus years, I'm totally convinced it is a Heaven-inspired book. In the midst of life's most painful struggles, aches, and pains, its soul-penetrating words and promises have brought real peace to my heart.

The Bible reveals a loving God who originally created a perfect Garden of Eden for both humans and animals. Without watering down reality, it describes the sin of Adam and Eve, its deadly effect on both man and beast, and also God's wonderful plan to restore Planet Earth to its original condition. Thankfully, if you peek at the final pages of the Bible, His love wins. A new earth is described in which will dwell both perfected people and many furry friends. The Good Book is very clear—both humans and animals will find a happy home in God's eternal kingdom. Read it for yourself:

For behold, I create new heavens and a new earth; and the former shall not be remembered or come to mind . . . The wolf and the lamb shall feed together, the lion shall eat straw like the ox . . . They shall not hurt nor destroy in all My holy mountain, says the Lord.

—ISAIAH 65:17,25)

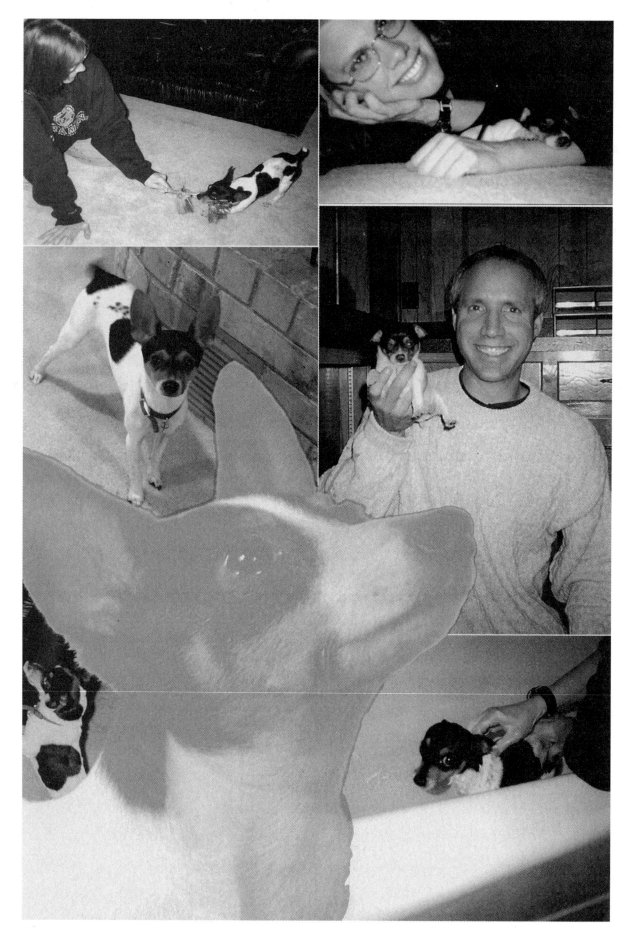

In the following pages of this book I will address the very real question asked by many aching hearts, "Will my pet go to heaven?" Yet from the get-go, just for the record, I must admit that no one knows with total, absolute certainty, except God Himself. So don't expect me to be super-dogmatic (pun intended). And if there's a slight chance you are concerned about Steve Wohlberg drifting off into some kind of pet-heresy, don't worry, I won't. I have been very careful to maintain scriptural sanity, reasonableness, and common sense. I promise you, there's nothing extreme, weird, or bizarre in here.

In addition—now don't miss this point!—I didn't write *Will My Pet Go to Heaven?* to ignite any animal arguments or cat controversies. So please don't get into any dog fights over this topic; it's not worth it. After you have finished reading this book, I'm confident you'll see it as an insightful, friendly work; totally sensible, and 100 percent kosher. But more important, you'll be surprised to find that it reveals many unexpected, deep, and power-packed truths that may even change your life.

I'm about to open my heart to you and to share an extremely traumatic and painful journey my wife Kristin and I passed through after the loss of a tiny friend. You will also learn my reasons—from the Bible, no less—why we have come to embrace the hope of someday seeing our dog's happy face again. Above all, if your own heart is open, you are going to discover many surprising and wonderful insights into the character of our heavenly Friend. Here lies my ultimate reason for writing this book. I hope to direct the hearts of animal-loving human beings toward a truly magnificent and super-loving Creator who cares for us all.

I hope to see you in His eternal kingdom.

More Readers Respond . . .
. . . to *Will My Pet Go to Heaven?*

You were so brave to write about the tragic death of your little Jax. Many of us are grateful that this inspired you to research the topic of pets in heaven.
Joan Fernish,
Spokane, WA

Dear Steve, I just read your book in one sitting. I loved it! I have had dogs and cats in my home all my life (I'm a 68-year old grandma now), so I've had to say goodbye many times. You NEVER get used to it. Two of the many dogs I've shared my home with were extra special (Cookie, my Boxer, and Chippy, my mini-Poodle). Right now I have an eleven-year-old Toy Fox Terrier who is almost identical to your Jax except bigger. . . . This book was a wonderful thing you did and it never would have happened without Jax. He served a tremendous purpose. God used him to lead you to write a book that gives hope and comfort to soooo many.
Thank you,
Donna Costa,
Port St. Lucie, FL

13. Our Dog's Name Was Jax

*I once had a sparrow alight upon my shoulder for a moment,
while I was hoeing in a village garden, and I felt that I was more
distinguished by that circumstance than I should have been by any epau-
let I could have worn.*

—HENRY DAVID THOREAU (1817–1862)

"Will Steve Wohlberg ever get married?" my closest friends had wondered for years. Even my parents were starting to doubt. But finally, at the ripe age of 41, I shocked them all by saying, "I do," in the presence of hundreds of guests inside a large church in California. Neither Kristin—formerly Kristin Renee Demarest—nor I had ever been married before, and this was the very special beginning of our new life together. The hit song, "You've Only Just Begun," applied perfectly. For years I had lived alone in tiny apartments, but now it was time for a house. In January of 2000, a few days after the much-feared Y2K glitch became the new millennium's most famous fizzle, I purchased a house for my new bride in a rather cozy residential section in Fort Worth, Texas. This was our first home.

It took me forty-one years to get married, and at this point I wasn't quite ready for any little Wohlbergs running around, so we decided to get a dog. Kristin liked the idea of a little one, and soon we found Jax. His original owners, Mark and Cortney Cooper, lived in the country just outside of Fort Worth. Because we are all very close friends, my wife and I often visit their home, sometimes even staying over on weekends. As a result of a certain circumstance, their little Jax needed a new home. One day, as the four of us talked about how Kristin and I were on the lookout for a pet, and they were searching for new owners, the fit seemed perfect. So Jax became our first dog.

*Dogs come when they're called;
cats take a message and get back to you later.*

—MARY BLY

Officially, Jax was a Toy Rat Terrier. These "toy" dogs are quite small, and even when fully grown, they're not normally more than six to eight pounds In addition, Jax was a runt, which means he was the smallest of his litter. He was about two years old when we placed him in my Ford Explorer to come home with us.

When we took him in, Jax wasn't sure if we were friends or foes. As a two-year-old in a strange house with new "parents," he panicked just a bit. During our first absence, we later discovered he had scratched up the windowsill near a rear door in the sunroom trying to get out. Maybe he wasn't sure whether we were coming back or not. He did this for three or four days each time we left. Yet Jax was a highly intelligent little guy. Each time we went away, he soon realized we did come back. After a few days of nurture, love, and a few fanny-whacks, he quickly settled down and became the almost-perfect dog.

The sound of birds stops the noise in my mind.
—CARLY SIMON (B. 1945)

When Kristin or I drove up to our house, Jax was often watching for us from the bay window near the front door. As we walked in, he would dance around in circles in the funniest way! He always wanted to be with us. In whatever room we entered, he was there. One time Kristin went into her clothes closet just for a minute, left, and closed the door. Later she walked back in and found Jax! Often as I sat in front of my computer he would gently kick me with his paw as if to say, "Please let me up!" At night we would pick him up and plop him on our bed. As Kristin and I prayed together, we would often add, ". . . and Lord, thank you also for our little Jax!" When the lights went out, our furry friend would slip under the covers and snuggle up close.

During the months that followed, our attachment for Jax deepened. I often thought, *What a great dog!* He was so cute-looking that when we took him out for walks on his little leash to a small lake near our home, cars would sometimes slow down, and those inside would point as if to say, "Look at that little fella!" Everyone liked him. He was friendly to our guests, played with their kids, and would sometimes just race around the house in a big circle just because he was happy. He had his favorite little rope, which he would often grab and shake like a toy. He became so much a part of our family that Kristin's mother once called and asked, "How's my grand-dog?" Our home is a Christian home—which included me, Kristin, Jesus, and of course, Jax.

Those were wonderful days.

14. The Day Tragedy Struck

Until one has loved an animal, a part of one's soul
remains unawakened.

—Anatole France (1844–1924)

Jax lived with us for almost a year. One Saturday evening, on October 27, 2001, the three of us drove out to visit with Mark, Cortney, and a group of other friends at their home in the country. The event was called, "The Fall Festival." It was a night of pleasant interaction, bonfires, and hayrides. We stayed the night, and, of course, Jax slept with us. On Sunday morning, our "little boy" stuck to us like glue, not wanting to get left behind. In retrospect, I wish we had left him. In any event, at about 2:00 P.M., we headed south toward our home in Fort Worth. As usual, Jax sat on Kristin's lap and licked the window for most of the trip. That was the last happy car ride he would ever take.

I parked the Explorer right in front of our home, alongside the curb, facing east. As I got out, Jax jumped out with me. As I walked to the back of the vehicle to get our bags, Jax skipped around with me and then onto our grassy lawn toward our front door. As I reached for our things, I glanced to my right and saw him happily prancing around near my wife. At that very moment my heart felt such joy. I remember this distinctly. *I sure love that dog!* were my exact thoughts. As I turned back to the car to grab our bags, it was right then that tragedy struck!

The mother eagle teaches her little ones to fly by making their nest
so uncomfortable that they are forced to leave it and commit
themselves to the unknown world of air outside.
And just so does our God to us. He stirs up our comfortable nests, and
pushes us over the edge of them, and we are forced to use our wings to
save ourselves from fatal falling. Read your trials in this light, and see if
you cannot begin to get a glimpse of their meaning. Your wings are being
developed.

—Hannah Whithall Smith (1832–1911)

I'll never forget it, at least not in this life. I didn't see it coming, but another SUV rounded the corner in front of me and drove right past me on my left side just a few feet from our car. "Jax!" Kristin screamed. I immediately turned to my left and saw his little yapping form dart underneath the other car. In a split-second of sheer horror I saw my tiny friend moving to bite the large left rear tire from underneath. I think he was trying to protect me, but he was no match for such a gigantic machine. As his tiny teeth bit the wheel near its front, the force of its forward-circular-downward motion quickly rammed his little head brutally into the ground. The car drove on, its driver never even knowing what had happened. So there Jax lay, motionless on the hot concrete, as if dead.

It may sound unbelievable, but in my 42 years of living, I have hardly ever felt such pain! "He's gone!" I yelled to my wife. As the tears gushed out, I had to look away. Just then another car came from the opposite direction right toward Jax as he lay bleeding in the middle of the street. I bolted out in front of the car, waved both of my arms frantically, and shouted wildly, "No! . . . Please! . . . Stop!" The lady stopped, and after saying, "I'm so, so sorry!" she drove carefully around two sobbing "parents."

It was an absolute nightmare. In the midst of the street, I knelt in front of our dog and moaned loudly, "Oh, Jax! Why did you do that? Why? Why? Why!" I was devastated. Then all of a sudden Kristin cried out, "Steve, he's moving!" My first thought was, *How horrible! Now I'll have to kill him so he won't suffer.* "Let's take him to the vet!" Kristin yelled. With a sense of utter hopelessness, I complied. I ran into the house, grabbed a towel, rushed back outside, and sadly wrapped Jax up. As we got into the car, I placed him on Kristin's lap. Then we raced away.

On the way to the vet, Jax started writhing and wiggling. "He's in his death struggle! You take him!" Kristin pleaded. So we switched places, and she drove. We went to two animal hospitals, but no one was there on a Sunday. Fortunately, on our third try, we found Dr. Morris and his wife doing some clean-up work at the Southwestern Animal Clinic of Fort Worth. By this time Jax was really squirming around, yet obviously without consciousness. The side of his face was bleeding, his neck seemed out of whack, and his eyes showed no sign of seeing anything. "I'll need to run some tests," Dr. Morris said after giving Jax a sedative. "Go home. I'll call you in a couple of hours."

In my heart, somewhere, a flicker of hope sprang up.

15. From Sunday to Wednesday

My little dog—a heartbeat at my feet.

—EDITH WHARTON (1862–1937)

The phone rang at about 5:30 that same Sunday afternoon. I was almost afraid to answer it. *Is Jax dead?* I wondered. "This is Dr. Morris. We've x-rayed his entire body, and he has no broken bones or fractures. But he definitely has a concussion, and his tiny brain is swollen. I'll call you again at about 9:00 tonight. That's it for now. Goodbye."

When I heard those words, everything in me knew it was time for prayer. "God, I know he's just a little dog, but, he's all we have. We have grown to love him so much! You made him, so please, please, save his life!" The next three days were quite amazing. This may sound silly, but we started a prayer chain for our little dog.

On Monday morning I was back at the vet's, and by this time I was starting to feel like a father visiting his sick child in the hospital! Our little dog had improved slightly, although not significantly. Mostly, he just lay on the table, twitching and jerking. By Tuesday, though, he was calmer, and even able to hold his head up. "He sometimes lifts his head and seems to look at me as I walk by his cage," the nurse remarked. "Once I even saw him twirling around on his front legs, trying to walk."

Come on Jax, you can make it! I thought. Yet his eyes showed little responsiveness.

"We hope that in a few days, after the swelling goes down in his brain, his mind will come back," she explained.

"Is it OK if I say a prayer in here?"

An animal's eyes have the power to speak a great language.

—MARTIN BUBER (1878–1965)

"Sure," the lady replied. So I drew close to his little ear and breathed out a few words to God. Amazingly, immediately after my prayer, Jax lifted his little head, turned, and looked right at me!

On Tuesday he remained stable, with additional slight improvements. After counseling with Dr. Morris, Kristin and I decided that on Wednesday afternoon we would take him home in hopes that, through being with us once again, he might muster his dwindling life forces and stage a super-Jax-comeback. After all, he was a tough little dog! Because he wasn't able to eat by himself, his nurses were feeding him intravenously. "He'll be fed, hydrated, and ready when you come back tomorrow."

Sadly, I drove home.

16. Halloween: Night of Death

There was a handsome male mockingbird that sang his heart out every morning during the nesting season from the top of a tall Norfolk pine tree. Last week the tree was cut down. The mockingbird and his song are gone. I can't put a dollar value on the tree nor on the mockingbird nor on his song. But I know that I—and our whole neighborhood—have suffered a loss. I wouldn't know how to count it in dollars.

—JACQUELYN HILLER

With a tightening knot in my stomach, Kristin and I drove back to the clinic on Wednesday afternoon at about 4:30. When the nurse brought Jax out and placed him in my arms, not much had changed. He was still stable, though a bit thinner, with one really glassy eye. Our plan was to take him home and then, after an hour or so, to have Mark and Cortney join us. By surrounding Jax with quadruple love, we all hoped he might revive.

We pulled up in front of our house, the scene of the accident. Walking past the exact spot where his head hit the ground three days earlier, I slowly and gently carried Jax in my arms through the front door. "You're back, Jax! Smell your doggie food, isn't it familiar? Here's our bedroom, remember? Now we're in your favorite room—the sunroom! See that squirrel outside the window? You always liked to bark at it. Jax, can you hear us? Jax! We love you!" No response. It was heartbreaking.

I laid him gently on a blanket on the floor near the center of the sunroom, and soon Mark and Cortney arrived. Then something astonishing happened. As the four of us gathered close around his tiny doggie body, Jax distinctly moaned once, then again. "He knows we're here," Mark said. "He wants to respond, but he can't. He's in pain."

We call them dumb animals, and so they are, for they cannot tell us how they feel, but they do not suffer less because they have no words.

—ANNA SEWELL, AUTHOR OF BLACK BEAUTY (1820–1878)

Before I left to go to our Wednesday night prayer meeting, we all knelt sadly beside our dog's motionless head. "Dear God, we love Jax so much, and we know You love him, too. Please, if it's Your will, heal him. If not, let him rest in peace. Oh God, give us a sign, one way or another, so we'll know what to do! We place his frail life in Your hands. In Jesus' name we pray, Amen." The reason I asked for a sign is because we didn't know how long we should try to maintain his existence if he didn't recover. Jax hadn't left us a will with instructions on when to pull the plug. Then I left for church.

Leading out in prayer meeting was very difficult that night. My heart ached, and my legs were weak. I finally told the group what was happening, and the name "Jax" was added to our prayer list. After my closing remarks a lady said to me, "I know of a German Shepherd who was hit on the head by an oncoming train. He was knocked out for weeks, but he recovered! Don't give up hope!" I hadn't, and I was soon heading back to Kristin, Mark, and Cortney.

When I walked into our house I found they had moved Jax into the living room. "His legs were getting cold," Kristin said quietly. It was about 9:00 P.M. We all sat around the living room and talked for a while. Then I went over to Jax and felt his legs. "He's getting colder," I said softly as I grabbed a few more blankets. His breathing also seemed quieter. Something was happening, I could feel it. His little body was closing down. "I think he's dying," I whispered.

Hear and bless Thy beasts and singing birds, and guard with tenderness, small things that have no words.
—AUTHOR UNKNOWN

The Nightly News came on at 10:00 P.M. Terrorism and Anthrax were the top stories. Then the usual stock market report. I don't remember if the NASDAQ went up or down. After that, some local news. It was Halloween evening, and the reports were positive. All was quiet, with no major events in Fort Worth. A few kids had come by and knocked on our door, but we were hardly in the mood even to answer. Kristin had planned to give out little boxes of raisins that night, but she forgot to buy them at a market down the street.

When the Nightly News was over, at about 10:30 P.M., I rose from the couch and walked over to Jax. He was lying by the fireplace, completely still. His eyes were still open. I pulled off the blankets, and slowly reached for his fast-cooling body. Nothing. No movement at all. I shook him slightly. Still nothing. Mark moved over and felt near his heart. "He's dead." I then picked Jax up and held his face close to mine. I lit a match and held it near his mouth. No flicker. "Yes. He's gone." We cried, and accepted this as God's will. Then I kissed my tiny friend for the last time.

As I look back on the events of that night, it all seems so amazing. Jax had been stable for three days. When we brought him home, his distinct moan told us he knew we were there. It was as if he wanted so badly to say, "Yes! I hear you! I love you, too! I'm trying to respond, but I can't!" It was as if he were trapped inside a broken brain. We had prayed, and even asked for a sign, then we trusted our "little boy" to our Father's heart.

The mystery of love is greater than the mystery of death.
—AUTHOR UNKNOWN

In retrospect, I really think Jax made a decision to die. Maybe this was the only way he could respond to us. He was finally home in our house, away from the strange clinic, and he knew it. The four human beings who loved him the most were there by his side. After our prayer, within a very short time, his body shut down, and that was it. We wrapped his small lifeless form in a blanket, put it in a box, and placed it in our cold garage.

Mark and Cortney decided to stay the night. In the morning I sadly placed the box in their pickup truck, and they took him out to their country property to bury him. That's where Jax grew up. His tiny grave is still there today.

17. My Personal Search Begins

I was gratified to be able to answer promptly.
I said, "I don't know."
—MARK TWAIN (1835–1910)

The next day after Jax died, I sadly sat down at my Hewlett-Packard desktop computer to send out some e-mail to a few friends who I knew had been praying for our dog. After opening up Microsoft Outlook, I brought up the first letter. With great difficulty I typed into the subject line, J A X I S D E A D. It was awful. At this point, I didn't have the slightest thought about ever seeing him again, and certainly not about writing this book! Yes, people had asked me before, "Steve, do you think our pets might be in heaven?" but I hadn't taken the question very seriously. After sending the first e-mail, I did the usual copy-and-paste thing. One by one, I clicked "Send."

Within a short time, a good friend from Canada responded with a rather unexpected note. He basically said, "After Jesus Christ comes, you'll see Jax again in a new doggie body!" What a nice thought, I mused. But still, I didn't take it seriously. Why should I? The central focus of the Bible is God, people, and human salvation, not dogs and cats, right?

Then a second friend from Alaska who had been praying for Jax e-mailed me back. This young man has a wife, two children, and two cats. Unknown to me, he was a great animal lover. In an attempt to give comfort, he not only expressed his personal hope that we might someday see our pets again, but then he gave this reason: He said our loving God just might bring them back to life again as a gift for those who are saved. Somehow, the five little words—for those who are saved—really affected me. Mysteriously, they struck a new note inside my soul.

A wise old owl sat in an oak.
The more he saw the less he spoke.
The less he spoke the more he heard.
Now wasn't he a wise old bird?
—AUTHOR UNKNOWN

For the next few moments I just sat there stunned, staring silently at my computer monitor. Could it be? Suddenly, something deep inside my heart seemed to change. Part of the pain was lifted. I sensed a very definite and loving presence draw near. I have felt this presence many times throughout the course of my spiritual journey, but never in this context.

Just then, an unexpected feeling of hope sprang up! "It's time for some research into a new topic!" I told myself.

18. God Loves Animals, Too!

*Not even a sparrow, worth only half a penny, can fall to the ground
without your Father knowing it.*

—JESUS CHRIST (MATTHEW 10:29 NLT)

In the last few years, I have written a number of fast-selling books and have traveled extensively speaking on Bible topics, especially the mysterious prophecies of the book of Revelation. My ministry has also taken me into the arena of radio and international television. I think it's safe to say that among my readers, listeners, and viewers, I've developed a reputation for presenting credible and well-researched information. But after Jax died, I entered an entirely new field of study. I wanted to see what the Bible might have to say about animals!

I was amazed at what I found. Going back to Genesis (the Bible's very first book), I carefully reexamined the creation account. Chapter 1 describes how God made everything by simply speaking. Then chapter 2 becomes more personal as Moses related how "the Lord God formed man from the dust of the earth" (v. 7). This showed me God's special interest in man. OK, but what about the animals?

*But now ask the beasts, and they will teach you;
And the birds of the air, and they will tell you;
Or speak to the earth, and it will teach you;
And the fish of the sea will explain to you.
Who among all these does not know
That the hand of the Lord has done this,
In whose hand is the life of every living thing,
And the breath of all mankind?*

—JOB 12:7-10

Then I read, "Out of the ground the Lord God formed every beast of the field . . ." (v. 19). This taught me that God not only carefully crafted man out of the earth, but also that He made the animals from the same chunk of ground. It's true, only man was created in the image of God (1:26), yet the animals were also purposefully and specifically "formed" by Him. I was impressed with a number of things. First, the very idea of "animals" came from God Himself. He conceived of, designed, built, and then brought them to life. Second, all animals are therefore primarily God's animals, for He made them. Third, He cares for them, or else why spend heavenly time and divine energy forming them at all?

"Out of the ground the Lord God formed every beast of the field and every bird of the air, and brought them to Adam to see what he would call them. And whatever Adam called each living creature, that was its name. So Adam gave names to all cattle, to the birds of the air, and to every beast of the field" (2:19, 20). This was even more interesting! A light went on in my head. I realized that in the Bible, which is the most important book ever written, one of the very first assignments God gave to man after He formed him was to name animals!

Just think of it! How exciting it must have been for Adam to find himself suddenly surrounded by an entire group of fuzzy, furry, woolly, feathery, purring, yapping, cooing, chirping, happy creatures! Then I thought, Why did God make these creatures in the first place? Upon further reflection, the answer seemed rather simple.

Originally, God didn't make His creatures to be killed and processed into McDonald's hamburgers or Kentucky Fried Chicken. Not at all. This only came later, and is the result of man's sin. Instead, the Lord made them because He is an intensely creative, highly personal, and extremely loving God (1 John 4:8) who simply wanted to enhance Adam's happiness and enjoyment. In other words, the animals were initially created by God to be man's friends, not his food: his pets, not his pork chops. So the Lord made them, and brought them to Adam. I imagine He said something like, "Here are some new friends! Now give them names." Later, Eve came along, but that's another story.

When Adam and Eve sinned in Genesis 3, God's original plan was shattered, and His whole creation was affected. Thankfully, His love for human beings didn't change one bit. But what about the animals? Does the Lord still care for them, even after the fall? In the midst of my is-there-hope-for-Jax research, I soon turned to the small book of Jonah. As I leafed through the pages, three words stuck out. Before, I'd hardly noticed them, but now they practically jumped off the page!

At the very end of this most unusual story, Jonah became upset because God decided not to punish the wicked, party-crazed city of Nineveh after all because its inhabitants had responded to His warning. In a merciful response to His unreasonable prophet, the Lord inquired, "Should I not pity Nineveh, that great city, in which are more than one hundred and twenty thousand persons who cannot discern between their right hand and their left—*and much livestock?*" (Jonah 4:11, italics added).

How marvelous! God not only pitied those sin-loving, disoriented humans in the city of Nineveh, but He also felt compassion for the mooing cows, baaing sheep, and bleating goats! These three words, "and much livestock," revealed to me God's tender love and compassion for even the animals that lived there. Think about it. If He cared back then, don't you think He still pities the pets in New York, Los Angeles, Russia, Afghanistan, and all over the world? Of course He does, for the Good Book says He is "the same yesterday, today, and forever" (Hebrews 13:8).

O Lord, you preserve both man and beast.
—Psalm 36:6

As my research continued, I discovered another Bible story that really touched my heart. As with the book of Jonah, I'd read it before, but now I was ripe for another fresh insight from our heavenly Friend. It was the story of a prophet-gone-bad named Balaam who abused his faithful donkey. As the two of them trotted down an isolated and dusty road, a holy angel with an unsheathed sword suddenly stood before them both, yet only the donkey saw him. Three times the donkey veered off the path to save his master's life. Finding his animal's actions totally unexplainable, Balaam cruelly reacted three times with a kick and a fist.

Finally the angel became visible to the eyes of the astonished prophet. "The angel of the Lord said to Balaam, 'Why have you struck your donkey these three times?'" (Numbers 22:32). Here we see a heavenly angel visiting earth and rebuking a human for his unreasonable harshness toward his four-legged friend! Besides this, after complimenting the heroic efforts of the donkey, the angel said to Balaam, "If she had not turned aside from me, surely I would also have killed you by now, and *let her live*" (v. 33, italics added). As a writer who likes to use his imagination, I could almost picture this headline, "Heavenly Being Kills Man but Saves Animal Alive." As with Genesis and the story of Jonah, another "click" occurred inside my mental computer. Not only does God love animals, but so do His angels.

I soon discovered that even the Ten Commandments reveal God's care for animals. The fourth commandment says,

Remember the Sabbath day, to keep it holy. Six days you shall labor and do all your work, but the seventh day is the Sabbath of the Lord your God, in it you shall do no work: you, nor your son, nor your daughter, nor your male servant, nor your female servant, nor your cattle, nor your stranger who is within your gates. For in six days the Lord made the heavens and the earth, the sea, and all that is in them, and rested on the seventh day. Therefore the Lord blessed the Sabbath day, and hallowed it.
—EXODUS 20:8-11, ITALICS ADDED

The fourth commandment reveals God as the all-powerful Creator of heaven and earth. After making Planet Earth in six literal, twenty-four-hour days, God rested on the seventh day. His law commands us to cease from secular work on the Sabbath so we can focus on our Maker, meditate on His creative power revealed in nature, and above all, get to know Him better. Yet it's not only people who are to rest. If you look closely, God's love extends even to the mooing cows, for they also are to take a break from plowing the fields (v. 10).

The Bible says the Ten Commandments were "written with the finger of God" on two tables of stone (Exodus 31:18). This shows the permanent nature of this law. Therefore the words, *nor your cattle* (v. 10), being indelibly carved into solid rock by God Himself, demonstrate the Almighty's permanent interest in animals. Yet there's more. If you think about it, that tiny and often overlooked phrase, *nor your cattle,* being part of God's moral law, also raises the issue of man's treatment of animals to a moral level. *Nor your cattle* ultimately means that human beings have a certain moral obligation to care for the needs of God's animals, and to treat them kindly.

A righteous man regards the life of his animal.
—PROVERBS 12:10

The biblical truth about our Creator is of mega-importance. It also contains hidden depths. The Bible's last and most mysterious book—"The Revelation"—reveals a special end-time message emphasizing this very truth. It is to be communicated "to every nation, tribe, tongue and people" before the second coming of Jesus Christ (Revelation 14:6, 14-16). This high-impact, life-and-death message proclaims, "Worship Him *who made heaven and earth, the sea and springs of water*" (v. 7, italics added).

Let's go deeper. Who specifically is the One who made heaven and earth—that is, the Milky Way, earth's continents, the Pacific Ocean, the Nile River, the animals in the San Diego Zoo, and everything else in existence? A careful study of the New Testament reveals it was actually Jesus Christ, who is "equal with God" (Philippians 2:6). The Bible says that our heavenly Father "created all things *through Jesus Christ*" (Ephesians 3:9, italics added).

A horse is an angel without wings.
—Author Unknown

Notice carefully: "He [Jesus Christ] was in the world, and the world was made *by him*, and the world knew him not" (John 1:10, KJV, italics added). Did you catch that? The power-packed message of this simple verse is that the Bethlehem Baby was really the Creator Himself coming to earth in the form of a human being. So what does this mean to us animal lovers? Simply this: It means that every dog, cat, bird, horse, dolphin—or any other creature—was actually thoughtfully designed, purposefully planned, and uniquely created by the very same One who ultimately gave His life on a splintery cross! In other words, all animals are really Jesus Christ's animals. He made them, He loves them, and they're His pets, too.

The Lord says,

For every beast of the forest is mine, and the cattle on a thousand hills. I know all the birds of the mountains, And the wild beasts of the field are mine.
—Psalm 50:10,11 italics added

"The Lord is good to all, and His tender mercies are over all His works" (Psalm 145:9). Our Lord has "tender" thoughts toward "all" His works, which certainly would include His animals. Now ask yourself this question: Whenever a human being's beloved dog, cat, bird, or horse gets hit by a car, drowns, dies from some disease, or simply wastes away from old age, does their Maker feel no pain? Their earthly owners do. Why is this? The answer is simple, yet profound. The reason is because human beings were made in the image of God, and the Lord suffers, too. If we who are in God's image feel such grief over the loss of an animal we have grown to love, then surely our pain must reveal a unique window into His heavenly heart.

I was really shocked to discover the depths of feeling that pulsated through my own aching heart when our tiny Rat Terrier died. In the days that followed, Kristin and I suffered a lot. It was hard to see that certain brown pillow on the couch in our living room on which Jax loved to sit. It brought tears to my eyes to see his little bowl still filled with Jax-food in the kitchen. And then there was that little Jax-photo of his doggie face on our dresser in the master bedroom. For many days, as we walked around the house, we imagined him everywhere! Everything seemed so unreal. Was he really gone, or was this a bad dream? Then I thought, Where do such feelings come from, anyway? As hard as it was, I learned a mega-lesson about God's love through my grief. The lesson was: He cares more than we realize—even for Jax.

Before I close this chapter, I want to share one more precious insight about God's love, not for animals, but for people. Look carefully at these words: "For the invisible things of him from

the creation of the world are clearly seen, being understood by the things that are made" (Romans 1:20). Get it? Paul said we understand "the invisible things" of God's character by looking at "the things that are made." In other words, God reveals aspects of His personality to us through His created works. That's why, in addition to the Bible, nature is called His second book.

God "made" Jax, right? When he was alive, every time I came home—and I mean every time—he could hardly wait to jump and start licking me! In my mind's eye I can still see his stubby tail wiggling. The more I think about it, our dog's love was ever-constant, even after those rare occasions when I had to spank his terrier-fanny for pooping or peeing on the carpet. No matter what, his love remained. Truly, Jax was a super-affectionate dog.

After his death I thought about his doggie-love more distinctly. Where did such love come from, anyway? Surely, it came from God. Our Creator made his wiggling tail, licking tongue, and loving heart. Why did He make these things in the first place? There can be only one answer. The reason is because God's "invisible" heart must be filled with wonderful love, and He must have chosen to reveal a portion of that love through His animals. Maybe that's why Moses wrote so long ago, "But now ask the beasts, and they will teach you" (Job 12:7).

Therefore, when any friendly creature of God—be it a dog, a cat, a bird, or a horse—prances, purrs, chirps, yaps, licks, snuggles, or tries to love us in any way, something fantastic is happening. We may not understand it, and it may roll right past us like the proverbial water off a duck's back, but we are witnessing a tiny glimpse of a super-creative and all-wise Creator's personal love for us through one of His love letters.

A meow massages the heart.
—STUART MCMILLAN

So the next time your horse gently nudges you, or your cat snuggles up against you, or a little puppy licks you, or your fully-grown faithful friend barks to protect you from danger, just think about this: Someone in heaven may be trying to say, "I love you," through your pet.

19. Will My Pet Go to Heaven?

I never meant you to be
Dog of My Heart,
But without speech you spoke to me,
Without hands you touched me,
Without reproach you humbled me.
And while I know there would have never been
A long-enough life, or the right time to say good-bye,
I will wait, however long it takes,
To get beyond my miserable state of grief and pain,
Towards warm and comforting
Remembrance,
And gratitude,
For the joy you brought me,
For the truths you taught me.

I never meant you to be
Dog of My Heart,
I only meant for you to mean as much.
But you meant
So much more.

—LILLIAN SUGAHARA (B. 1955)

Is there any hope for Jax?" I asked myself seriously. I know, he was just a dog, but Kristin and I had come to love that tiny ball of fur. Now that I had definite proof from the Bible that God not only created and loves His animals, but even reveals a portion of His own love through them, I decided to look for other passages that might reveal the possibility—however remote—that we might someday see our little dancing, funny friend again.

In this chapter I am going to share with you the results of my search and journey. As I said before, I can't say for sure whether our pets will be in heaven. Ultimately, that's up to God. The Bible doesn't say in black and white, "Your dog, cat, or horse will someday have wings." Nevertheless, I have found some very significant passages which I think do suggest the strong possibility that at least some of this world's sin-suffering animals might transition over to "the other side." Of course, you must come to your own conclusion.

First, the Bible does plainly teach that a new world is coming. The very last Bible writer,

whose name was John, declared, "I saw a new heaven and a new earth, for the first heaven and the first earth had passed away . . . And God will wipe away every tear from their eyes; there shall be no more death, nor sorrow, nor crying. There shall be no more pain, for the former things have passed away" (Rev. 21:1, 4). Peter also wrote, "Nevertheless we, according to His promise, look for new heavens and a new earth in which righteousness dwells" (2 Peter 3:13).

In that happy place there'll be no more terrorist hijackers, suicide bombers, heart disease, arthritis, pain, smog, or taxes to pay to the IRS. We also have the assurance that animals will be there, too. The Good Book says, "The wolf also shall dwell with the lamb, the leopard shall lie down with the young goat, the calf and the young lion and the fatling together; and a little child shall lead them . . . They shall not hurt nor destroy in all My holy mountain, for the earth shall be full of the knowledge of the glory of the Lord as the waters cover the sea" (Isaiah 11:6, 9).

Therefore, according to 2 Peter 3 and Isaiah 11, not only will saved human beings be there, but so will wolves, lions, leopards, goats, and probably lots of other animals. In that wonderful place, wolves won't snarl, lions won't bite, and leopards won't be scary. God's promise is, "They shall not hurt nor destroy in all My holy mountain." Won't that be great?

It seems to me that when it comes to those future kingdom-creatures, God has three options:

Option #1: He can create entirely new animals from scratch.

Option #2: He can bring back to life animals that have suffered in our present world, giving them immortal bodies.

Option #3: He can make some new animals and bring back some old ones as well.

Unless there is some unrevealed factor preventing Him from doing so, I think the all-powerful God can accomplish any or all of these options. His Word says, "Behold, I am the Lord, the God of all flesh. Is there anything too hard for me?" (Jeremiah 32:27). If God wants to re-create in the new world some of the animals from this old world, it's an easy task. Besides, by then He will have already accomplished something much more dramatic—the resurrection of all the dead human beings.

Jesus Christ said, "Do not marvel at this; for the hour is coming in which all who are in the graves will hear His voice and come forth . . ." (John 5:28, 29). At His second coming, "many of those who sleep in the dust of the earth shall awake . . ." (Daniel 12:2). "For the trumpet will sound, and the dead will be raised incorruptible, and we shall be changed" (1 Corinthians 15:52). Therefore, if God has the supernatural turbo-power to resurrect dead human beings at the return of Jesus Christ, then surely He has the ability to bring back to life a mini-dog named Jax in His new earth if He so chooses. It would be as easy as snapping His fingers.

During my pet search, a gentle voice behind my mind seemed to whisper, "Read Romans 8." I had read this chapter before, but now something beckoned toward a closer look. After paging my way to this New Testament section, this is what I found:

> *For the earnest expectation of the creature eagerly waiteth for the manifestation of the sons of God. For the creature was made subject to vanity, not willingly, but by reason of him who hath subjected the same in hope. Because the creature itself also shall be delivered from the bondage of corruption into the glorious liberty of the children of God. For we know that the whole creation groaneth and travaileth in pain together until now. And not only they, but ourselves also, which have the firstfruits of the Spirit, even we ourselves groan within ourselves, waiting for the adoption . . . the redemption of our body.*
>
> —ROMANS 8:19-23

These words deserve careful consideration. In fact, this has become one of my main there-might-be-hope-for-Jax sections. In my Bible prophecy seminars, I always encourage my audiences to put away preconceived opinions and to pay close attention to the text—to the actual words of God. Only then can we really understand the message of truth. If we look closely at Romans 8:19-23, the concepts are truly amazing.

Paul revealed how Adam's sin affected the "whole creation" (v. 22), which must include the animals, too. Yet sin will not continue forever. In the interim, the "creature itself" (v. 21) is portrayed as "eagerly waiting" (v. 19), in "hope" (v. 20), while yet "groaning . . . in pain" (v. 22) until the full restoration after the second coming of Jesus Christ. Then "the creature itself also shall be delivered from the bondage of corruption into the glorious liberty of the children of God" (v. 21).

Did you catch that? After the return of Jesus Christ even "the creature itself *also* shall be *delivered*" (v. 21, italics added). To me, the words "also . . . delivered" seem to reveal the positive transition of Planet Earth and at least some of it's creatures from one state to another. The first state is one of bondage, corruption, and pain as a result of Adam's sin. The second state—after the second coming of Jesus Christ—is one in which "the creature [creation] itself" will also be delivered from this very corruption in order to share in the "glorious liberty of the children of God." It seems to me that Romans 8:19-23 implies that at least some of the creatures in this sinful world will be delivered from their present suffering resulting from man's sin and transported into the new earth.

That's a pretty powerful passage, isn't it? But guess what? There's an even better Bible section that gives me hope for Jax. In fact, if it wasn't for the discovery of this super-unique

Bible passage, this book might not have been written. As we examine these verses, you be the judge. They're definitely about animals, their deaths, and their return to the dust. But then—at least it seems this way to me—they also talk about how God will bring them back to life again!

Of all the creatures God made at the Creation, there is none more excellent or so much to be respected, as a horse.

—BEDOUIN LEGEND

These amazing verses are found in Psalm 104. It's a Psalm of God's works, of His creation, and of His wonderful care for both man and animals. Written by King David, Psalm 104 mentions every beast of the field and the wild donkeys (v. 11), the birds (v. 12), the cattle (v. 14), the wild goats (v. 18), rock badgers (v. 18), living things both small and great (v. 25), the young lions (v. 21) and finally, man (v. 23). Ecstatic about God's creativity and His tender care for all His creatures, David burst forth with joy, "O Lord, how manifold are Your works! In wisdom You have made them all. The earth is full of Your possessions" (v. 24).

Read the following words very carefully:

These all wait for You, that You may give them their food in due season. What You give them they gather in; You open your hand, they are filled with good. You hide your face, they are troubled; You take away their breath, they die and return to their dust. You send forth Your Spirit, they are created; And You renew the face of the earth. May the glory of the Lord endure forever; May the Lord rejoice in His works.

—PSALM 104:27-31

With a sense of awe I read that section again and again. *Wow!* was my exact thought. In the spirit of honest inquiry and with a true desire to accurately discover what the Bible really says, I will list five points worth considering:

1. Psalm 104 definitely concerns both man and animals.

2. The death of animals is described: "You take away their breath, they die, and return to their dust" (v. 29).

3. Then David seems to describe God bringing back to life at least some of the very ones that have died: "You send forth Your Spirit, they are created" (v. 30). Again, "*they* die . . . *they* are created" (Italics added).

4. This passage seems to point forward to the time of the new earth, for David continues, ". . . they are created, and You renew the face of the earth." This renewal also seems to parallel a New Testament prediction about how, after the second coming of Jesus Christ, there will come "the times of restoration of all things, which God has spoken by the mouth of all His holy prophets since the world began" (Acts 3:20, 21).

5. Finally, Psalm 104:31 looks into eternity with the triumphant shout, "May the glory of the Lord endure forever; May the Lord rejoice in His works."

After reading verse 31, I thought to myself, Wasn't Jax one of God's works? Didn't the Lord create him and keep his little doggie heart beating for three happy years? And what about all those endearing and funny qualities that touched our hearts—wasn't God Himself the author of every positive personality trait?

Of course, when God finally does create a new earth during "the times of restoration of all things," He surely has the option of making another dog comparable to Jax, or no dogs at all for that matter. But then again, why not restore to life that same little five-pound ball of fur? It makes sense to me that He might do this. Psalm 104 does say, "they die . . . they are created, and You renew the face of the earth" (v. 31). The bottom line is, whatever God ultimately decides, Psalm 104 gives me another reason to hope in the possibility that I might see Jax again.

Then another thought popped into my head, What about God's promise to answer our prayers? The Lord says, "Call to Me, and I will answer you" (Jeremiah 33:3). People often ask God for things and then watch Him "answer." Sometimes we pray for major things like forgiveness for some sin, for victory over powerful temptations, for guidance in choosing a marriage partner, for relatives who don't know His love, etc., etc. We also pray for smaller, more personal things like passing a school exam, for a virus-infected computer to start functioning again, for weight-loss assistance, for help in finding lost car keys, etc., etc. A real Christian is a praying Christian, and real Christians often thank God for large as well as tiny answers to prayer.

As I was studying the Word and grieving over Jax, I thought to myself, *God has answered so many of my prayers, so what's wrong with asking Him to bring Jax back to life someday?* Jesus even said, "If you then, being evil, know how to give good gifts to your children, how much more will your Father who is in heaven give good things to those who ask Him!" (Matthew 7:11). Then I pondered, *Wouldn't seeing Jax again be a good thing?* It seemed so. Again I thought, If I had infinite power, wouldn't I give this good gift to my child? So shortly thereafter, Kristin and I knelt down in our sunroom and prayed a special, focused prayer to our loving heavenly Father in the name of His Son, Jesus Christ. I don't remember exactly what we said, but it was something like,

"Dear God, we really loved Jax, and we know You loved him, too. After all, he was one of Your works. The Bible says You do answer prayer, and so we ask You this specifically: When You finally do remake the heavens and the earth, if it's Your will, please bring Jax back to life so we can see him again. In Jesus' name we pray, Amen."

I'm sure the good Lord heard that prayer, and so did His angels. It's a fact—a formal prayer from two sincere believers about a dog named Jax was lodged that day before the throne of the King of the universe. We trust our Father's heart. Ultimately, it's up to Him. We really hope He chooses to answer our humble request.

At the beginning of this book I listed some stories about how animals have rescued lost children or adults who had fallen into danger. Some of these tales are intensely dramatic, even worth reporting on CNN. Do you think God Himself might be involved behind the scenes in some of these stories? I do. In fact, the Bible itself records how God sent a bird to feed the prophet Elijah so he wouldn't die in the desert (1 Kings 17:4). Yes, God sometimes does mobilize His non-human creatures to help or save people in need, and I imagine that some of these rescue operations come as a direct answer to the prayers of humans.

To the dolphin alone, nature has given that which the best philosophers seek: Friendship for no advantage. Though it has no need of help from any man, it is a genial friend to all and has helped mankind.

—PLUTARCH (CIRCA A.D. 45–125)

In this light, is it so unthinkable that God might answer the prayer of a human by recreating a much-loved pet in the new earth, simply because we ask Him to? Concerning the resurrection of Jesus Christ, Paul said, "Why should it be thought a thing incredible with you, that God should raise the dead?" (Acts 26:8, KJV). God is a miracle-worker. If He can resurrect the dead, then surely He can bring a tiny dog back to life. The Lord loves people and animals, and He definitely answers prayer. Will He answer our Jax-prayer? We hope so.

"For with God nothing will be impossible." Luke 1:37. The Almighty made Planet Earth in one literal week (Genesis 1 and 2). He opened the Red Sea for the Israelites to pass through (Exodus 14) and shook the ground of Mount Sinai (Exodus 19 and 20) when He gave the Ten Commandments. He later caused the sun to stand still for Joshua (Joshua 10). During the reign of Persia, He shut the mouths of hungry lions so they wouldn't eat his friend Daniel for supper (Daniel 6).

The greatest miracle of all occurred approximately 2,000 years ago. The Eternal One even incarnated Himself into tiny microscopic cells inside the body of Mary (John 1:1-3,14; Matthew 1:23). Jesus Christ was born, grew up, lived, suffered, and died on a cruel cross to demonstrate God's love for man and to atone for our sins. Then on the third day He rose from the dead (Matthew 28:5, 6).

In view of such stupendous miracles, doesn't the Almighty have the power to re-create a tiny dog named Jax if He wants to?

I think so.

20. Mysteries of Heaven's Lamb

Man, do not pride yourself on superiority to animals; they are without sin, and you, with your greatness, defile the earth by your appearance on it, and leave the traces of your foulness after you—alas, it is true of almost every one of us!

—Fyodor Dostoyevsky (1821–1881)

One of the themes of this book is that God not only loves people, but animals, too. After all, He created their beating hearts, intricate brains, breathing lungs, and functioning livers—plus their mysterious and almost human-like ability to suffer, cry, and even love. Yet for many animal lovers who read the Bible, a difficult question arises: If God cares so much for all His creatures, then why did He command Adam, Abel, Noah, Moses, King David, and millions of Jews to slice the throats of friendly lambs?

In order to understand this painful and repulsive practice, we must again go back to the book of Genesis. The Holy Book begins with this simple and majestic sentence: "In the beginning God created the heavens and the earth" (Genesis 1:1). On the first day He made the light (v. 3). On the second day He spread out the blue sky (v. 8). On the third day He formed Planet Earth itself with its peacefully rolling sea (v. 13). On the fourth day He made the brilliant sun, the reflecting moon, and all the shining stars (v. 16). On day five He spoke the colorful birds and numerous sea creatures into existence (v. 20). Then on the sixth day . . . Presto! . . . He formed the animals and then man (vv. 25 and 26).

"Then God said, 'Let us make man in Our image, according to Our likeness . . .'" (1:26). How marvelous! We didn't evolve from slime, goop, sludge, quadrupeds, mollusks, fish, or apes. Definitely not! The Bible says an all-powerful Creator—a God of love—originally made human beings in His own likeness. Thus the first man began with two legs, not four. His name was Adam, and his wife was called Eve. Then God placed our first parents in a beautiful garden called Eden.

Eden was a happy place, graced with crystal-clear rivers, colorful flowers, magnificent trees, smog-free air, and yes, lots of furry, four-legged, friendly animals. Yet in the very midst of this perfect paradise grew a forbidden tree, "the tree of the knowledge of good and evil" (2:17). The Bible reveals that in His infinite wisdom, God made this tree to test the love and loyalty of Adam and Eve for their Maker. Did they appreciate the gift of life from the Almighty Giver? Were they thankful to have each other as companions? Did they appreciate even the furry animals He created to add to their happiness and enjoyment? Love for their all-gracious Maker—this was the core issue.

"The Lord God commanded the man, saying, 'You are free to eat from every tree of the garden. But you shall not eat of the tree of the knowledge of good and evil. For in the day you eat of it, you will surely die'" (2:16, 17). There it is, God's test of love, and His awesome warning of death if they purposefully chose to disobey. Amazingly, Adam and Eve failed the test! A highly intelligent, super-tricky enemy seduced them from their loyalty (see 3:1-6). Eve "took of its fruit and ate. She also gave to her husband with her, and he ate" (3:6). This infamous act of ingratitude and rebellion against the expressed will of their Maker was not only wrong, but deadly. In the Bible, that act is given this name: Sin. Sin is serious.

"Through one man sin entered the world, and death through sin" (Romans 5:12). You may have a hard time believing this, but all of Earth's present problems, including the horrors of the Nazi Holocaust, the nightmare of starvation in Africa, the evil of child-abuse, the intense pain of September 11, 2001, and even the comparatively insignificant death of a small rat terrier named Jax—these are all ultimately rooted in that one bitter bite of forbidden fruit.

So what was a loving God to do? Should He allow Adam and Eve to perish in their sins, or implement a plan for their salvation? Fortunately for us, God chose the latter. Because death was the divine penalty for sin, His special plan out of necessity also involved death, even the death of His Son. That's why the Bible not only says, "The wages of sin is death" but also, "the gift of God is eternal life in Christ Jesus our Lord" (6:23).

Here's a very important question. How did God decide to powerfully illustrate His unique plan for our salvation? The answer is: Through the death of His animals!

Try to imagine this scene. A humble Jewish family has a little lamb that their children named Softy. He's so cute; they treat him like a pet. The kids love him, feed him, and sometimes even sleep with him. Yet one day their dad takes Softy away.

"Where's our little lamb?" the children ask their mom.

"Your father took him to the Temple."

"Oh . . . well . . . when are they coming back?" the kids ask nervously.

A tear forms in Mom's eyes, she holds the boys close and whispers, "Boys, Softy is not coming back . . ."

Leading Softy with a rope, the father arrives at the Temple and slowly approaches the altar of sacrifice. Softy isn't afraid, for he trusts his owner. After gently positioning the timid creature in front of him, dad places his quivering hand on the animal's unsuspecting head, much like a man would stroke his pet. He confesses his sins over it, representing the transfer of those sins to the innocent victim. A specially-robed priest then hands the father a razor-sharp knife, which he quietly slips under its woolly throat. The lamb tenses slightly, and swallows. Beads of sweat form on the man's head as his heart races wildly. Finally, the man closes his eyes and says a prayer. "Baa," says the lamb. In the next in-

stant there is a horrific groan as the knife is plunged into the animal's warm flesh and as its blood spurts and pours. Softy's eyes roll upward in that moment of shock and terror, and it's over.

All we like sheep have gone astray; We have turned, every one, to his own way; And the Lord has laid on him the sin of us all.
—ISAIAH 53:6

In this awful ceremony—repeated millions of times in Jewish history—God was teaching the human race both the Bad News and the Good News. The Bad News is that sin is more serious than we realize, and its penalty is death. But the Good News is that our loving Creator decided to come to earth as a man and to offer His own life as a perfect sacrifice in our place.

The ancient Jewish prophets predicted that the Savior would come. Micah said His birthplace would be in Bethlehem (Micah 5:2). Isaiah said He would be like "a lamb led to the slaughter" (Isaiah 53:7). When Jesus Christ finally appeared on earth after thousands of years of sin, sorrow, and animal sacrifices, a prophet named John shouted loudly, "Behold! The Lamb of God

who takes away the sin of the world!" (John 1:29). The perfect sacrificial lamb had come in the person of Jesus Christ.

After Jax died, in the midst of my animal research, I was increasingly struck by the definite Jesus-animal connection revealed in the prophecies and described in the New Testament. In fact, the very last book of the Bible refers many times to Jesus as the Lamb (see Revelation 5:6,12; 6:1; 7:17; 13:8; 14:1,10; 15:3; 17:14; 19:9; 21:21; 22:1). Thus the Bible not only uses an animal to represent Jesus Christ, but this is also the primary symbol for Him in the book of Revelation.

Why a lamb? I pondered. Why illustrate Christ's sacrifice by the death of an innocent creature? Suddenly the answer burst upon me like sunlight from behind a cloud. From the very beginning in Eden, God must have created human beings and the more intelligent animals with a certain capacity to lovingly bond with each other. Remember, one of the very first things God did after He made Adam was to surround him with animals so he could name them. Thus the animals were originally created to be man's companions and friends. In other words, God designed human hearts and animal hearts to mysteriously connect.

After Adam and Eve foolishly fell away from their Creator, the Lord wanted to reveal to the whole human race the seriousness of sin, His plan of salvation, His desire to win our hearts. So what was the best way He could think of to accomplish these goals? The incredible answer is: By telling human beings to take the very animals they were naturally designed to love, and to kill them!

It was hard enough to watch Jax get hit by a car and to see him bleeding in the street. But what if God told me to take a knife myself and slit his throat? I could hardly do it. It would be extremely difficult and painful. Almost impossible. But that's the point. By telling man to take an innocent, woolly, friendly animal—a lamb—and then to kill it with his own bare hands, this was God's way of trying to show us how horrible sin is and how awesome is the infinite sacrifice of Jesus Christ. "Kill the lamb," God commanded, "and realize it represents my Son who will die in your place for your sins." Such a painful, high-impact revelation should melt our hearts with His love and also lead us to turn away from our sins!

Paul wrote, "For I delivered to you first of all that which I also received: that Christ died for our sins according to the Scriptures, and that He was buried, and that He rose again the third day according to the Scriptures" (1 Corinthians 15:3, 4). This is the Good News in a nutshell. Jesus is our sin-bearer, our all-sufficient sacrifice—the final sacrifice (Hebrews 10:12).

We can easily forgive a child who is afraid of the dark. The real tragedy of life is when men are afraid of the light.
—PLATO (427–347 B.C.)

Have you ever had to euthanize your favorite dog, cat, bird, monkey, sheep, goat, or horse? A close friend of mine who is married and has two small children put his only dog to sleep recently. "It was one of the hardest things I ever did!" he moaned. In a sense, that's exactly what the heavenly Father did to His Son on the cross two thousand years ago. But Jesus Christ had to die so we could live.

For God so loved the world that He gave His only begotten Son, that whoever believes in Him should not perish but have everlasting life.
—JOHN 3:16

How should we respond to such love? The Bible clearly says we should:

1. "Repent," which means to confess and forsake our sins (Proverbs 28:13; Luke 13:3, 5; Acts 2:38; 1 John 1:9).

2. Believe in Jesus Christ as our Savior instead of relying on our own goodness, works, or merits for eternal salvation (John 3:16; Ephesians 2:8, 9).

3. Trust fully in God's grace and free forgiveness for every sin (1 John 1:9; Romans 4:7, 8).

4. Receive by faith the power of His Holy Spirit into our hearts (Acts 1:8; Romans 5:5).

5. Because we love Him, live moral lives by the grace of God in harmony with the Ten Commandments (John 14:15; Titus 2:11,12; Revelation 12:17; 14:12).

6. Wait patiently for the second coming of Jesus Christ (Matthew 24:30, 31, 44; Titus 2:13; Revelation 14:14-16).

7. Look forward to God's new earth (2 Peter 3:13; Revelation 21:1-5).

After Jax died I read God's book, the Bible. The truth became so clear to me. I understood His desire for us to love His animals. I also knew why He said, "The lambs must die!" Then I saw *the Lamb,* and our loving God's perfect plan to win our hearts.

Twenty-three years ago I gave my heart to God. It was the best decision I've ever made.

21. Dead Dogs Don't Bark!

A lie can travel halfway around the world while the truth is putting on its shoes.

—MARK TWAIN (1835–1910)

"Why did you write that unusual chapter, *Dead Dogs Don't Bark?*" the producer of one of the programs on Billy Graham's *Decision Today* radio network asked me right before an interview about this book. "I know, it's different," I said, "But believe it or not, many grieving pet owners today are not only pondering whether or not their deceased animal is still alive somewhere, but even whether their four-legged friend might somehow be able to communicate with them from the other side."

In my Jax-research I discovered this to be true and was surprised to discover numerous accounts of individuals who claim that the spirit of their dead pet actually appeared to them from beyond the grave. Because of this growing trend, I decided to address this topic.

The Pets That Returned[35]

"Mr. Gerald Mills lives in the Northern town of Sheffield, Yorkshire, UK. He has owned many pets during his lifetime, but two have been extra special. This is his extraordinary story:

"Some years ago I was working in a factory in Sheffield when I noticed a little black kitten that was lost and on its own. The poor thing was covered in dirt and oil from the factory floor where it had been living. In truth I thought it would not live long as it was so weak when I found it. But I took it home and gave it some warm milk and a tiny bit of fish I had in the fridge. Then I placed it in an old shoe box with some clean dusters to keep it warm. The next morning the little kitten was still alive and looking at me as though I were its best friend. Well I suppose I was in a way. So I fed it some more milk and the cat purred so softly. I was really taken with it and gave it a name. I called the cat, Tiger, because it had stripes and was obviously a brave kitten.

"I already owned a dog called Suzy and soon Tiger and she were real pals. It was fun to watch them playing together. They were like that for many years, Tiger and Suzy side by side sitting in front of our coal fire, best of friends.

"Years passed by so swiftly, it hardly seemed any time at all since I first found that kitten. Tiger and Suzy had grown old together and now, as God would have it, they both became ill at the same time. I tried to nurse them, but it was time and rather than see them suffering I took both Tiger and Suzy to the veterinary surgeon. I held them in my arms as he helped them to pass over into the spirit world.

"It was some two years later that I noticed something strange at the foot of my bed. I was

almost asleep when I first felt it, a kind of snuggly thing pressing against my feet. Immediately I thought of Tiger, she would often fall asleep on my bed and snuggle up near the foot of my bed. Looking down towards where I felt the pressure on my feet I saw, to my amazement, a cat. It was the spirit of Tiger come back from beyond to comfort me.

"As I stared in wonder at the 'ghost' of Tiger I heard a strange but familiar sound coming from downstairs. It sounded just like the barking of a dog. As I listened I recognized the bark as being that of my old friend Suzy. She too had returned to wish me well and let me know that in the future, when it is my turn to walk forward into the world of spirit, my pets will be there to welcome me. They were together still, Suzy and Tiger, alive and well in their spirit bodies."[36]

This is not an isolated incident. John G. Sutton is the author of the book, *Psychic Pets: Supernatural True Stories of Paranormal Animals*. One of the chapters in John's book entitled, "Gypsy the Singing Cat," contains a non-fiction account of "a cat voice" that supposedly sang "from beyond the grave."[37] I also came across another popular book called, *Ghost Dogs of the South,*[38] which has this summary statement on its publishers' website advertising its contents:

Digging deeply through the rich field of Southern folklore, the authors have discovered that a dog's devotion to its human does not always end at the grave. Dogs can be as peculiar as people. Their relationship with humans is complex. In story after story from Southern homes, there is strong evidence that this relationship can extend beyond death. Do dogs return from the other side to comfort and aid their human companions? You bet your buried bones they do.[39]

I'm sure you're aware that there are lots of so-called spiritualists, mediums, and psychics out there who claim the ability to communicate with the dead. But did you know that some of these profess an ability to contact not only those who had two legs, but also those with four? And with the increasing popularity of books such as *The New York Times* bestseller *Talking to Heaven: A Medium's Message of Life after Death*.[40] New Age radio programs such as "The Next Dimension," and psychic TV shows such as "Crossing Over" with John Edward and "The Pet Psychic," it seems the temptation is growing for more and more pet-grieving seekers to try and contact Fuzzy or Fido again.

In my research I also located the website of Carla Person, a woman who features herself as a "Shamanic Healer and Animal Communicator," and one who definitely claims the psychic ability to contact our dead pets. On her internet home page I found this listed as one of the services she offers her many clients: "Learn how your special

friend is doing in the afterlife, if/when she will return, and what messages she has for you."[41]

Here's something to think about: How come you never see a headline like "Psychic Wins Lottery"?

—JAY LENO (B. 1950)

Whenever a favorite animal dies, it's natural to wish it was still here. Kristin and I have been there and done that. This really, really hurts. But is it realistic to believe our dead pets are yet alive somewhere beyond our realm of time and space? In other words, have they now passed over into some spirit world? Can their ghosts still bark, baa, neigh, or purr? Do animals have separate souls that can exit their furry bodies, fly upward to heaven, and then go back and forth between up there and down here, appearing or disappearing at will?

First of all, the Bible nowhere says that animals in this sinful world are by nature immortal, that they have separately conscious spirit-souls capable of leaving their bodies, or that these invisible, intelligent entities float upward to heaven when they die. And there is definitely no "word from the Lord" in the Scriptures about any pet-ghosts making noises from beyond the grave. It's true, animals do have what the Bible calls "the breath of life" or "the breath of the spirit of life" (see Genesis 7:15, 21, 22; Psalm 104:29, 30), but this breath or spirit is not an internally intelligent entity capable of exiting animal bodies, hovering over pet-graves, watching pet-funeral services, and later meowing in response to the beckoning of a spirit medium.

In fact, the Bible actually forbids all forms of attempted communication with those who have died, which, in principle, would certainly apply to God's lesser creatures. When the Israelites were about to enter the Land of Promise, the Lord strictly warned:

> When you come into the land which the Lord your God is giving you, you shall not learn to follow the abominations of those nations. There shall not be found among you anyone who makes his son or daughter pass through the fire, or one who practices witchcraft, or a soothsayer, or one who interprets omens, or a sorcerer, or one who conjures spells, or *a medium, or a spiritist, or one who calls up the dead.* For all who do these things are an abomination to the Lord, and because of these abominations the Lord your God drives them out from before you. You shall be blameless before the Lord your God.
> —Deuteronomy 18:9–13, italics added

I realize these are strong words, but God knows they are needed. The reason for this counsel is because the Lord desires to protect His children, not just from the deception of phony psychics, but also from contact with real spirits. These may seem friendly, but their hidden agenda is not our happiness. Remember the super-tricky, highly-intelligent, invisible enemy who seduced Adam and Eve into sin? (see Genesis 3:1–6). Well, he still exists, and so do his angels. The Bible refers to this sinister being as "that serpent of old, called the Devil and Satan, who deceives the whole world; he was cast out into the earth, and his angels were cast out with him" (Revelation 12:9).

In an age of universal deceit, telling the truth is a revolutionary act.
—GEORGE ORWELL (1903–1950)

God's Holy Book has much to say about mediums and familiar spirits (Leviticus 20:6), and it's not positive. These things are placed in the same category as witchcraft (2 Kings 21:6). Biblically speaking, a familiar spirit is a spirit or ghost from the other side that looks, acts, and talks in a familiar way. These spirits usually take the form of dead humans, such as one's cousin Ralph or aunt Suzie. Based on books like *Psychic Pets, Ghost Dogs From the South,* and the spiritualistic activities of people such as Carla Person, it seems they can even look like Fido.

But honestly, "familiarity" is not reality. Based on God's Word, we can safely say they are clever impersonations. These friendly-looking spirits are really dangerous fallen angels in league with Lucifer. The book of Revelation lifts the veil on these beings, saying, "They are the spirits of devils, working miracles" (Revelation 16:14). Therefore, just as the Titanic should have steered clear of the iceberg, even so should we steer clear of all mysterious beyond-the-grave human ghosts or pet spirits. On the other hand, we should know that real angels like the ones that spoke to Balaam, the virgin Mary, and Peter do sometimes appear in order to advance God's purpose (see Numbers 22:22-35; Luke 1:26-38; Acts 12:5-11).

Before I close this chapter, I want to clarify the basic biblical timeline so you can understand exactly when a person might hope to see a favorite pet again.

1. The Creation—God made a perfect garden in Eden for both human beings and animals (Genesis 1 and 2).

2. The Fall of Man—When Adam and Eve were seduced into sin by a beautiful, brilliant, fallen angel named Lucifer who used a serpent as his medium (Genesis 3; Isaiah 14:12-14; Ezekiel 28:14, 15, 17; Revelation 12:9). As a result of sin, corruption and death entered our world, which also affected God's animals.

3. Fallen Human History—The zigzagging course of Planet Earth after sin entered (Genesis 6:5, 11, 12; Matthew 24:12-14). Animal sacrifices were initiated which pointed toward the future appearance and sacrificial death of the Lamb-Man, Jesus Christ (Genesis 3:21; 4:4).

4. The First Coming of Jesus Christ—The apex of God's awesome plan to save human beings from sin and death. On a cruel cross—Heaven's Ground Zero—the Lamb-Man died for the sins of the entire world (1 John 2:2). Jesus Christ was buried, rose again, and then ascended bodily to heaven (1 Corinthians 15:3, 4; Acts 1:9-11).

5. The Second Coming of Jesus Christ—The future climax of fallen human history. The Lamb-Man will return visibly at the end of this world (Matthew 24:14, 27, 30, 31, 44; 25:31, 32; 28:20).

6. The Resurrection of Dead Humans—There will be a final, literal, bodily resurrection of both the saved and the lost (Daniel 12:2; John 5:28, 29; Acts 24:15; 1 Thessalonians 4:16, 17; Revelation 20:4-6).

7. The Final Judgment—When human beings are held accountable for their personal sins of breaking God's moral law and even for their cruel mistreatment of His animals. The lost will then realize why they are lost; that is, because they have persistently turned away from their Maker, His love, and from the fullness of Jesus Christ's sacrifice (Daniel 7:9, 10; Ecclesiastes 12:13, 14; John 3:16-21; Revelation 20:11-13).

I tremble for my species when I reflect that God is just.
—THOMAS JEFFERSON (1743–1826)

8. Earth's Final Purification by Fire—In an awesome act of incredible majesty and infinite power, the Almighty will use high-temperature flames to completely cleanse Planet Earth from all the toxic effects of sin and Satan (2 Peter 3:7, 10; Revelation 20:14, 15).

9. The New Earth—After the final sanitizing of this sin-polluted earth and it's smog-infected atmosphere, God will wondrously remake the heavens and the earth to restore life as it was in the beginning (2 Peter 3:10-13; Revelation 20:15; 21:1).

10. The Creation of New Animals—In His New Earth, the Lord God will once again create four-legged, friendly animals as loving companions for eternally saved human beings. But because sin will never occur again, these animals will never die (Isaiah 11:6, 9; 65:17, 25; Nahum 1:9).

I want to stress that it will be in the New Earth that God will once again create His animals. And these kingdom-pets will not be floating spirits that soar down from heaven into perfect animal bodies. Not at all. If we stick with the Bible, there's no real evidence that our dead pets

are alive in heaven right now, and they certainly can't meow, bark, or woof at us from the other side. Thus the title of my book, *Will My Pet Go to Heaven?* biblically, realistically, and sensibly applies to God's New Earth, not to an immediate afterlife that may be entered at the moment of death.

As painful as it is for my wife and me, the fact is, Jax is dead, and his tiny grave lies just west of Fort Worth. This is part of the reality of sin. The Scripture says, "All go to one place: all are from the dust, and all return to the dust" (Ecclesiastes 3:20). But the good news is, sin won't last forever, and a new earth is coming. When heaven's clock finally ticks over to that time, there really is no biblical evidence that God will do anything other than what He did in the Garden of Eden, which was to form *"every beast* of the field . . . out of the ground" (Genesis 2:19, italics supplied). Therefore, just as in the past, God's future kingdom-creatures will come from the dust, not a spirit world. And it will be at this time that Kristin and I hope to see Jax again, if the good Lord is willing.

> *Let hundreds like me perish, but let TRUTH prevail.*
> —MAHATMA GANDHI (1869–1948)

No matter how popular the psychic radio programs and TV shows may be, I urge you to stay away from all mediums, paranormal psychic-communicators, and especially familiar spirits. If a ghostly apparition looks an awful lot like your grandpa Bill, your sister Martha, or even Snow Ball or Fido, don't interact with it; it is a lie.

I know the loss of any loved one is terribly hard. But really, the safest thing is to find solace in true earthly friends and in the living "God of all comfort" (2 Corinthians 1:3). Our heavenly Friend really cares, and He knows what it's like to lose a loved one. It happened to Him when His own Son died on a cross.

22. Pets, People, and Priorities

Of how much more value then is a man than a sheep?
—Jesus Christ (Matthew 12:12)

God loves our pets, and He wants us to love them, too. But when it comes to intrinsic value, one human being—just one—is more precious to the heavenly Father than all the dogs that ever barked, all the cats that ever purred, all the birds that ever chirped, all the sheep that ever went "baa," and all the horses that ever neighed. Jesus Christ says to each of us, "You are of *more value* than *many* sparrows" (Matthew 10:31, italics added). In fact, if you could be placed on a shelf with a price tag, it would read, "Cost: The life of God's Son!"

When Kristin and I went through the pain of losing Jax, behind it all, this thought kept echoing in my soul: If we care so much for a tiny terrier, how much more must God care for human beings? Jax died less than two months after terrorist hijackers destroyed the World Trade Center and crashed into the Pentagon. Compared to the loss of husbands, wives, sons, daughters, and close friends who died at Ground Zero or on those American and United flights, our dog's death was nearly insignificant.

This "Human Beings Have Priority" issue is easily proven by once again taking a closer look at the original creation week. As we have already seen, during the first four days God created the light, the sky, the earth, the sea, the sun, the moon, and the stars. On the fifth day He made the birds and the fish. During the first part of the sixth day He formed the animals. After that, as His final act of super-creative genius, "The Lord said, 'Let us make man in our image, after our likeness'" (Genesis 1:26). Thus man was made last, and he alone was formed in God's express image. In other words, God's crowning work had two legs, not four.

After Adam and Eve sinned, God's special plan was implemented for the specific purpose of saving humans, not animals. And as we saw earlier, throughout the Old Testament God was even willing to sacrifice animals to illustrate His plan. This fact alone should lead us to value people above pets. When Jesus Christ finally entered this world to offer His life as the ultimate sacrifice for sin, the Bible says, "Christ died for *us*" (Romans 5:8, italics added)—not for Fido, Fuzzy, or Black Beauty.

The more I think about the excruciating agony and infinite sacrifice of Jesus Christ to save human beings from sin and its attached penalty of eternal death, I must say that although I do appreciate the good deeds of the Humane Society, I value the work of the American Bible Society more. After His resurrection, Jesus didn't specifically tell His followers to "Go into all the world and rescue stray dogs," as important as this is. Instead, He commissioned, "Go into all the world and preach the gospel" (Mark 16:15).

Therefore, our primary energies should be centered on reaching out to disoriented, mixed-

up, lost human beings with the good news of the Savior who died for them. The fact is, our greatest happiness can never be found in an exclusive devotion to God's animals—even though sometimes they are easier to live with! Instead, it comes through discovering our Creator's love, in experiencing His awesome grace and forgiveness, and by a life of heartfelt service to other people created in His own image.

Too often we underestimate the power of a touch, a smile, a kind word, a listening ear, an honest compliment, or the smallest act of caring, all of which have the potential to turn a life around.

—LEO BUSCAGLIA (1924–1998)

It's awful to think about all the abandoned dogs that roam our streets without collars, yet a homeless child is worse. While it may be heart-sickening to imagine a crying puppy in the pound, how can this compare to the fading eyes of a starving boy or girl? While we may rejoice when a favorite cat hit by a Toyota recovers, what is this compared to the deliverance of a child-abused heroin addict from New York who surrenders his life to God's power? While God may smile when an Arabian horse's half-broken ankle heals, Jesus Christ taught that there is greater "joy in the presence of the angels of God over one sinner who repents" (Luke 15:10). In other words, when human beings repent down here, holy angels have a huge celebration up there!

Should we love the animals? Yes. Be kind to God's creatures? Of course. Enjoy their companionship? For sure. But let's never forget that the Creator of all life—in the form of a man—agonized, sweat drops of blood, wept, and died on a cruel cross for the specific purpose of bringing eternal life to human beings, not animals.

It's as simple as our ABCs. In the light of His infinite sacrifice, people come first, then pets.

Now, go do the right thing!

—DR. LAURA SCHLESSINGER

23. When Lions Don't Bite

In the Bible is a famous story about a man named Daniel who was thrown by his enemies into a den of man-eating lions. He's toast for sure, they thought. Yet after a pleasant night's sleep surrounded by furry "pillows," Daniel said, "My God sent His angel and shut the lions' mouths, so that they have not hurt me" (Daniel 6:22). The same God who had the power to make mean lions harmless has promised that some day, every lion will be as tame as your kitty cat.

The book of Revelation records:

> And I saw a new heaven and a new earth, for the first heaven and the first earth had passed away. . . . And God shall wipe away every tear from there eyes; there shall be no more death, nor sorrow, nor crying. There shall be no more pain, for the former things have passed away. Then He who sat on the throne said, "Behold, I make all things new." And He said to me, "Write, for these words are true and faithful." And He said to me, "It is done! I am the Alpha and the Omega, the Beginning and the End. I will give of the fountain of the water of life freely to him who thirsts"
> —Revelation 21:1, 4-6).

A new earth is coming. It will be a Garden of Eden restored. God says so, and His Word is true (verse 5). In that bright land, all who have been redeemed through the shed blood and spotless righteousness of Heaven's Lamb will never die. Beyond this, there'll be lots of happy animals jumping around there. With beyond-this-world vision, the ancient prophet Isaiah wrote:

> The wolf also shall dwell with the lamb, the leopard shall lie down with the young goat, The calf and the young lion and the fatling together; and a little child shall lead them . . . They shall not hurt nor destroy in all My holy mountain, for the earth shall be full of the knowledge of the Lord, as the waters cover the sea.
> —Isaiah 11:6, 9; 65:17, 25

How utterly fantastic! Pets forever! In that happy place, there'll be no more people funerals, pet funerals, grief recovery groups, or need for Therapy Dogs International, Inc. to send its K-9 troops to a latter-day Ground Zero.

Heaven is a city without a cemetery.
—AUTHOR UNKNOWN

What will it be like to befriend a wolf, take a stroll with a leopard, ride piggyback on a gentle

lion, or slide down the neck of a playful giraffe? Better yet, how would you like to be surrounded by a whole family of grizzly bears, without the slightest tinge of fear? Sounds like a dream, doesn't it? But it's true. God has promised, "These words are true and faithful" (Revelation 21:5).

A little girl from a smog-covered city went camping for the first time with her mother in the mountains. On their first night out, as the child stood outside their tent and looked up at the brilliant stars, she was amazed to see such beautiful dots instead of pollution and haze. "Oh, Mother," she reported excitedly, "If heaven is so beautiful on the wrong side, what must it be like on the right side!"

How true! In this life we can only imagine the heavenly kingdom. But someday the haze will vanish, and we will find ourselves in the midst of a perfect world with crystal-clear lakes, smog-free air, gorgeous flowers, pleasant hills, happy humans, and super-dazzling beauty.

Kristin and I are really looking forward to being there. And of course, we sincerely hope that one of our forever friends will be a tiny Rat Terrier named Jax, whose fragile heart stopped beating on a dreary Halloween evening in 2001. When the good Lord finally recreates a pollution-free planet—and when His creative voice, like thunder, once again proclaims something like, "Let the earth bring forth the living creature according to its kind" (Genesis 1:24)—we would love to see Jax reappear in a free-from-the-effects-of-sin, immortal, doggie body to dance, skip, prance, cuddle, and lick us once again. How wonderful this would be! Honestly, Kristin and I believe in the real possibility of this happening.

When it comes to the topic of our animals becoming kingdom-pets, I will now summarize the core concept of this book.

Our Creator is a highly personal and intensely loving God who originally formed His animals in the Garden of Eden to become friendly companions for human beings and to make them happy. In the galactic laboratory of His own eternal creativity, He not only designed human hearts to connect with each other and with Him, but He also added the extra blessing of fashioning human hearts and animal hearts in such a way that they would tenderly bond with each other.

As an integral part of this happy design, the good Lord specifically gave His more intelligent animals a certain capacity not only to think but also to love. This special ability—the ability to love—most definitely sets the higher animals apart from the lesser creatures.

Even after sin, our wonderful God continues to love both people and their pets, and He is not unmindful of the affectionate and tender relationships established between them. If He numbers the very hairs on our heads (Matthew 10:30), then surely He also knows the number of furry strands on Fido!

The Lord is also the supreme and all-powerful One to whom "nothing shall be impossible" (Luke 1:37). In light of the above concepts, which I consider to reflect solid, biblical facts, it seems to me both reasonable and possible that in the New

Earth, our loving God just might choose to snap His fingers, so to speak, and bring back to life certain animals that have become the special friends of His blood-bought children, to enhance their eternal happiness.

For me personally, after Jax died, the thought that God might bring my beloved pet back to me in eternity helped relieve my suffering heart. As this idea dawned upon my wounded soul, I began to sense the comfort of His presence.

Nevertheless, I must go on record as stating clearly that even if that same little pooch is not recreated, this will not change Kristin's or my love for God. We will still be satisfied, at peace, and happy. God's promise is: "And My people shall be satisfied with My goodness, says the Lord" (Jeremiah 31:14).

Above all—wonder of wonders!—Jesus Christ Himself will be there. With a tender heart, He'll explain everything that has confused us on "this side of the river." As we look into His loving face and see the remaining nail-scars in His hands and feet, there'll surely be no disappointment. Along with millions of other human beings redeemed by His heart-rending sacrifice, we will bask in His deep, untainted, infinite love forever. His love goes far beyond the love of any animal! Jesus proved His love on that dreary day so long ago on a hill outside Jerusalem, when His own heart stopped beating.

Will my pet go to heaven? I surely hope so. Yet by far the bigger question is: Will you and I go to heaven, along with our spouses, sons, daughters, parents, relatives, and those we love? As far as our beloved pets are concerned, the issue for them is simply whether or not God chooses to recreate them in His New Earth. But for us humans, the far larger issue is whether we choose to repent of our sins, to trust fully in Jesus Christ and His sacrifice (symbolized by all those slaughtered lambs), and to follow the plain teachings of the Bible. If we do, then by His grace, we'll be ready for His soon return and will have a home in Eden restored.

> Behold, I am coming quickly! Blessed is he who keeps the words of the prophecy of this book. . . . And the Spirit and the bride say, "Come!" And let him who hears say, "Come!" And let him who thirsts come. Whoever desires, let him take the water of life freely
> —Revelation 22:7; 22:17

> Then the King will say to those on His right hand, "Come, you blessed of My Father, inherit the kingdom prepared for you from the foundation of the world."
> —Matthew 25:34

As much as we love our animals, our own eternal life is more important than the destiny of our pets. In light of eternity—which is a very long, long, long time—it's a no-brainer, and making sure that we ourselves enter the "Land of no good-byes" should be our top priority. Bottom line: It's more important than puppy chow.

Kristin and I prayed really hard that Jax would live. When his glassy eyes finally faded into unseeing darkness, our aching hearts questioned, "Oh God, why?" Maybe this book is part of His answer. If our compassionate Creator can use my words to touch even one human life and lead that life to a better understanding of His love and purposes, then our precious Jax did not die in vain.

By the way, we finally did get another dog. He's a super-cute Toy Rat Terrier who looks just like Jax! We named him Rerun.[42]

In the next and final chapter of this book, I'll share more Bible insights to help you make sure you'll be in God's kingdom with your best friend, Jesus Christ, with His redeemed people from all ages, and with His friendly animals.

24. The Key to the Kingdom

Man has no choice but to choose.
—JEAN PAUL SARTRE (1905 – 1980)

February 25, 2004, was the release date of Mel Gibson's extremely controversial film, *The Passion of the Christ*. Whether you saw the movie or not, millions did, and it became one of the most well-attended religious films in history. What was particularly interesting to me as I read about the heated discussions over whether Mel's *Passion* might contribute to anti-Semitism against innocent Jewish people or not, was the fact that in the midst of the fiery debate, even the secular media was exploring this vital question: *Who really was Jesus Christ, anyway?* A good man? More than a man? A prophet? More than a prophet? Was He the "Son of the living God" as He claimed—or a deluded fanatic?

Because I am a Jewish Christian author of eight books and one of the hosts of the radio program, *World News and the Bible*, we not only covered the subject ourselves, but I was interviewed on three radio shows immediately after *The Passion* opened in theatres. The hosts were anxious to hear my perspective. During each interview I brought up the core issue: The true identity of the Mystery Man who was cruelly beaten, violently scourged, and finally crucified between two thieves outside Jerusalem. Who was He? On the dark night of His trial, before His condemnation and death, Jesus of Nazareth was asked by the Jewish high priest, "I put you under oath by the living God: Tell us if you are the Christ, the Son of God" (Matthew 26:63). In suspenseful silence, the Sanhedrin waited for the Rejected One's response. "It is as you said," replied the innocent Sufferer, "Nevertheless, I say to you, hereafter you will see the Son of Man sitting at the right hand of the Power, and coming on the clouds of heaven" (Matthew 26:64).

"It is as you said," the Lord replied. According to the New Testament, the humble Carpenter is indeed the Christ, the Messiah, the Son of God, the "Savior of the world" (1 John 4:14). In His teaching, which held crowds spellbound, He plainly stated, "Most assuredly, I say to you, *he who believes in Me has everlasting life"* (John 6:47, emphasis added). "I am the resurrection and the life" (John 11:25). "For God so loved the world, that He gave His only Son, that whoever *believes in Him* should not perish but have everlasting life" (John 3:16, emphasis added).

According to the Controversial One, if we want to live beyond this short life on this earth—with its pain, sadness, and stress—we must believe in Him as our personal Savior and surrender

91

our hearts to His grace. The living issue is: Jesus Christ—and what we do with Him. *This will decide our destiny.*

After Jax died, Rerun became our favorite pet. One particular day when Kristin was gone, and I was caught up with important tasks in our home office, Rerun would not leave me alone. He kept whimpering for attention, but I couldn't spend time with him. I was just too busy.

"Not now, boy."

"Stop crying."

"Rerun—not now!"

After numerous frustrating "conversations" with my adorable but now nagging dog, I finally said, "Get out! Go! *Go Now!*" Each time I raised my voice, Rerun sheepishly took another reluctant step toward the door. "Go!" I shouted for the last time, as he slowly sulked down the hallway toward our bedroom.

After completing my tasks, and with a certain feeling of guilt, I sought him out, hoping he still loved me. I found him where he usually sat, inside the pillows on the master bed, on Kristin's side. As I approached, he propped his little head up and looked at me. "Rerun," I said softly, "I'm sorry, little guy." Then I saw what I was hoping for: The wag of his stubby tail, the flattened ears, and the final sign—the tummy turn. Yep, he still loved me, in spite of my shooing him away a few hours earlier.

As you look back on your life, can you remember times when you've turned someone away? I'm not talking about you favorite pet, but your Savior and Lord, the Crucified One, Jesus Christ, who gave His life for you. If so, you may be wondering *if He still loves you*, if He still wants you, if there is still any real hope for you personally to live forever with Him. Friend, there is! Yes, He loves you with His whole soul. That's why He willingly took the whip and the nails—yet more important—experienced our sin.

Beyond the physical pain that the real Jesus—not the actor in the movie—endured, there's a big lesson we can learn from Mel Gibson. Whatever your conclusions about this millionaire's life and character, there's one thing Mel did which contains a lesson for us all. Although he funded and directed *The Passion*, he refused to act in it, or even be seen—except in one scene. It was *his fist* holding the hammer which drove the nails into the hands of the man who played the Savior. "I wanted to make a statement to the world," Mr. Gibson reported, "that my sin put Him there."

How true! Not only does Jesus deeply love you and me, but we are all guilty of His death. Our sins put Him there—every one of us, both Jew and non-Jew. He paid the full price, made the complete sacrifice, and was buried in Joseph's tomb. Then He rose from the dead. His Jerusalem tomb is empty. Someday, He will return just as He promised, to "make all things new" (Revelation 21:5). While we wait, He alone can fill our empty, sin-scarred hearts with full forgiveness and love, *giving us assurance of eternal life.*

How can we prepare for the afterlife? What is the key to the kingdom?

The key is believing fully in the Mystery Man and in what He said to the high priest who inquired about His true identity—that He is indeed the Christ, the Son of the living God, the "Savior of the world" (1 John 4:14)—and in forsaking our sins.

And this is the testimony:
that God has given us eternal life,
and this life is in His Son. He who has the Son has life:
and he who does not have the Son of God does not have life.
—1 JOHN 5:11, 12

For the wages of sin is death,
but the gift of God is eternal life in Christ Jesus our Lord.
—ROMANS 6:23

If we confess our sins, He is faithful and just
to forgive us our sins, and to cleanse us from all unrighteousness.
—1 JOHN 1:9

Even to your old age, I am He,
And even to your gray hairs I will carry you!
I have made, and will bear;
Even I will carry, and will deliver you.
—ISAIAH 46:4

I urge you to respond to God's love, turn from sin, and believe in Jesus Christ as your best Friend and Saviour so we can meet on the other side.

Believe me, the retirement benefits Jesus offers us are out of this world.

Endnotes

1. *Newsweek:* Special Report—"After the Terror." September 24, 2001. Article entitled, "The End of the End of History," by Fareed Zakaria

2. Taken from the article, *Volunteers, The Spirit of America,* on TDI's website (see *www.tdi-dog.org/disaster.htm*). Paragraph by Nanette Winter, M.A., Director of Psychological Services, Northstar Industries, Saranac Lake, NY; TDI evaluator.

3. Also taken from the article, *Volunteers, The Spirit of America,* on TDI's website (see *www.tdi-dog.org/disaster.htm*).

4. Taken from *www.heinzdoghero.com*—a Heinz Pet Products website featuring their *Hero Dogs of the Year Awards: A Tribute to 47 Years of Amazing Canines.* For story details, click on "Timeline of Heroes."

5. Reported in an article by Lee Dye on *ABCNEWS.com*, October 2002. See *http://abcnews.go.com/sections/scitech/DyeHard/dyehard021010.html.*

6. For further information on Michigan State University's "Human-Animal Bond Initiative," see *http://nursing.msu.edu/habi/index.html.*

7. Listed under Delta Society Goals, taken from their website, *http://www.deltasociety.org/dsf000.htm#mission.*

8. Lee Dye's article on *ABCNEWS.com*, October 2002.

9. Gazella K., "Learning From the Heart." St. Petersburg *Times.* March 15, 2000.

10. For more information, visit their website at http://aahabv.org

11. PAWSitive InterAction. "Pets and the Aging: Science Supports the Human-Animal Bond." "White Paper" based on PAWSitive InterAction's Second Annual Summit. Atlanta, Georgia. 2003. Accessed at *www.pawsitiveinteraction.org.*

12. Schoen, A.M. "Kindred Spirits: How the Remarkable Bond Between Humans and Animals Can Change the Way We Live." New York: Broadway Books, 2001.

13. Becker, M. "The Healing Power of Pets: Harnessing the Amazing Ability of Pets to Make and Keep People Healthy and Happy." New York: Hyperion, 2002.

14. National Institutes of Health (NIH). "The health benefits of pets." NIH Technology Assessment Statement Online, 1987, Sep 10, 11. *http://odp.od.nih.gov/consensus/ta/003/003_statement.htm.* Accessed February 12, 2004.

15. Almqvist, *American Journal of Respiratory and Critical Care Medicine, 2001:* "Worsened asthma in kids from cats." Almqvist, C., Wickman, M., Perfetti, L., Berglind, N., Renstrom, A., Hedren, M., Larsson, K., Hedlin, G., Malmberg, P., "Worsening of asthma in children allergic to cats, after indirect exposure to cat at school," *American Journal of Respiratory and Critical Care Medicine,* 2001 Mar., 163(3 Pt 1):694-8.

16. Svanes C., Jarvis, D., Chinn, S., Burney, P., "Childhood environment and adult atopy: results from the European Community Respiratory Health Survey," *Journal of Allergy and Clinical Immunology,* 1999 Mar;103 (3 Pt 1):415-420.

17. Miyake, Y., Yokoyama, T., Yura, A., Iki, M., Shimizu, T., "Ecological association of water hardness with prevalence of childhood atopic dermatitis in a Japanese urban area." *Environ Res.* 2004 Jan;94(1):33-37.

18. McNally, N.J., Williams, H.C., Phillips, D.R., Smallman-Raynor, M., Lewis, S., Venn, A., Britton, J., "Atopic eczema and domestic water hardness." *Lancet,* 1998 Aug 15;352(9127):527-31.

19. Gonzalez-Quintela, A., Vidal, C., Gude, F., "Alcohol-induced alterations in serum immunoglobulin e (IgE) levels in human subjects." *Front Biosci.* 2002 May 1;7:e234-44.

20. National Institutes of Health (NIH). "The health benefits of pets," NIH Technology Assess Statement Online 1987 Sep 10, 11. *http://odp.od.nih.gov/consensus/ta/003/003_statement.htm.* Accessed February 12, 2004.

21. Headey, B., "Pet ownership: good for health?" *Med J Aust.* 2003 Nov 3;179(9):460-461.

22. McGinnis, J.M., Foege, W.H., "Actual causes of death in the United States," *JAMA.* 1993 Nov 10;270(18):2207-12.

23. Lee, C.D., Blair, S.N., Jackson, A.S., "Cardiorespiratory fitness, body composition, and all-cause and cardiovascular disease mortality in men," *Am J Clin Nutr.* 1999 Mar;69(3):373-80.

24. Blair, S.N., Cheng, Y., Holder, J.S., "Is physical activity or physical fitness more important in defining health benefits?" *Med Sci Sports Exerc.* 2001 Jun;33(6 Suppl):S379-99; discussion S419-20.

25. Nesby-O'Dell, S., Scanlon, K.S., Cogswell, M.E., Gillespie, C., Hollis, B.W., Looker, A.C., Allen, C., Doughertly, C., Gunter, E.W., Bowman, B.A., "Hypovitaminosis D prevalence and determinants among African American and white women of reproductive age: third National Health and Nutrition Examination Survey, 1988-1994," *Am J Clin Nutr.* 2002 Jul;76(1):187-92.

26. Holick, M.F.. "Too little vitamin D in premenopausal women: why should we care?" *Am J Clin Nutr.* 2002 Jul;76(1):3, 4.

27. Keller, H.H., McKenzie, J.D., "Nutritional risk in vulnerable community-living seniors," *Can J Diet Pract Res.* 2003 Winter; 64(4):195-201.
28. Roberts, W.C., *Am Heart J* 1995; 130:580-600.
29. Dickens, M., "Chapter IV" in *My Father As I Recall Him.* E.P.Dutton & Co.. New York, 1897.
30. Dowsett, R., Shannon, M.. "Childhood Plumbism Identified after Lead Poisoning in Household Pets," *N Engl J Med,* 1994 Dec 15; 331(24):1661-1662.
31. Morse, S., "New Distance Course In Companion Animal Behavior And Welfare," Animal News Center, 2004 Jan 13. *http://www.anc.org/pets/pets_article.cfm?identifier=2004_0113_edinburgh.*
32. Wood, D., "Does Anyone Know I'm Here?" *Guideposts,* 2002 July; 62(5):24-28.
33. Wineman, N.M., Schwetz, K.M., Zeller, R,, Cyphert, J., "Longitudinal analysis of illness uncertainty, coping, hopefulness, and mood during participation in a clinical drug trial," *J Neurosci Nurs* 01-Apr-2003; 35(2): 100-6.
34. Lissoni, P., Cangemi, P., Pirato, D., Roselli, M.G., Rovelli, F., Brivio, F., Malugani, F., Maestroni, G.J., Conti, A., Laudon, M., Malysheva, O., Giani, L., "A review on cancer—psychospiritual status interactions. *Neuroendocrinol Lett.* 2001 Jun;22(3): 175-80.
35. This story was taken from John G. Sutton, author of the book, *Psychic Pets: Supernatural True Stories of Paranormal Animals.* Beyond Words Publishing, Inc., 1998.
36. See *www.pyschicworld.net/ppp.htm.*
37. See *www.pyschicnet.net/Psychic%20Pets.htm.*
38. *Ghost Dogs of the South*, by Randy Russell and Janet Barnett. John F. Blair, Publisher (2001).
39. Taken from *www.blairpub.com/folklore/ghostdogssouth.htm*, the official website of John F. Blair, Publisher.
40. Talking to Heaven: A Medium's Message of Life After Death, by James Van Praagh. Penguin Putnam Inc. 2001.
41. See *www.spirithealer.com.*
42. On pages 48 and 49 of this book, all of the puppy pictures are of Rerun, as is the picture of the full-grown dog by the vent wagging his tail. All of the other dog photos are of Jax. The adults are Steve and Kristin Wohlberg.

STUDY THE BIBLE BY MAIL

FREE Discover Bible Study Guides help you find the answers to life's most important questions:

♦ SUFFERING—Why does God permit it? Does He really care?

♦ LIFE AFTER DEATH—What will it be like?

♦ PRAYER—How can I know God will hear and answer me?

♦ THE FUTURE—Is there hope for our troubled world?

Get your first lesson by clipping the form below and mailing to the address shown.

Name_____

Address_____

City_____ State____ Zip_____

Mail to:

DISCOVER
Box 53055
Los Angeles, CA 90053-0055